San Francisco Bay Guardian

Best Teatime

The English Rose Restaurant

"*Recipes are generally quick and easy to reproduce …engaging drawings.* —**The Bookwatch**

"*Step into the English Rose Restaurant for a visit to a charming tearoom from abroad. (Sheppard's) cookbook contains all the delicious dishes she serves in the restaurant.* —**Lou Pappas**

"*When an ethnic restaurant makes you nostalgic for the country it represents, it must be doing something right. **The English Rose** makes us long for the British Isles in a way few other local shops do.*
—**A Guide to the Bay Area's Best Ethnic Restaurants**

The English Rose Restaurant Cookbook

by Marilyn Sheppard

Wide World Publishing/Tetra

In order to help today's busy cook save time, the author has sometimes suggested packaged ingredients in some recipes.

Of course, you may modify as you wish.

Wide World Publishing/Tetra
P.O. Box 476
San Carlos, CA 94070

Revised Edition June 1999.

Printed in the United States of America.

Interior graphics by Marjorie Jackson

Library of Congress Cataloging-in-Publication Data

Sheppard, Marilyn, 1960-
    The English Rose Restaurant cookbook.

    Includes index.
    1. Cookery, English. 2. Cookery--California--
San Carlos. 3. English Rose Restaurant (San Carlos,
Calif.) I. Title
TX717.S473 1987   641.5'09794'69   88-17298
ISBN 1-884550-22-3

Dedicated with love and gratitude to my parents,
Stella and Tom Haslett,
for their never-ending support,
and
to my aunt, Joyce Thomas,
who got me started in the restaurant business.

Contents

SOUPS

CREAM of MUSHROOM SOUP

Beautiful soup! Who would not give all else for two pennyworth only of beautiful soup?

– Alice in Wonderland

2 T butter or margarine
3 T onion, chopped
2 1/2 cups mushrooms, finely
    chopped
2 T flour
3 cups chicken stock
3/4 cup half and half
Salt
White pepper

Melt butter in a medium saucepan over medium heat.
Add onion. Sauté until softened.
Add mushrooms. Sauté 5 minutes.
Stir in flour. Cook 1 minute, stirring constantly.
Gradually stir in stock. Bring to a boil.
Reduce heat. Simmer about 15 minutes until mushrooms are tender.
Stir in half and half when ready to serve. Season with salt and pepper to taste.
Reheat.
Serves 6.

CREAM of BRUSSELS SPROUTS SOUP

1 lb. Brussels sprouts
4 T butter
1 onion, chopped
4 cups chicken stock
Salt and pepper
Whipping cream or half and half

Cut the sprouts in half. Wash carefully.
Sauté onion in butter until softened.
Add sprouts. Simmer for a few minutes.
Add chicken stock. Simmer until sprouts are soft.
Purée. Add salt and pepper to taste.
Add cream or half and half when ready to serve.
Reheat.
Serves 4.

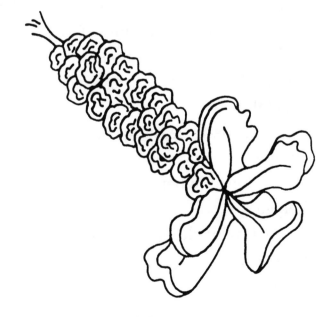

POTATO-LEEK SOUP

3 T oil
3 T butter or margarine
4 cups leeks, sliced
4 pounds unpeeled potatoes, chopped
2 small rutabagas or turnips, peeled and chopped
1 pound carrots, chopped
1/2 pound mushrooms, chopped
3 quarts chicken stock
1 t salt
1/2 t white pepper
Whipping cream or half and half
Parsley, chopped

Sauté leeks in oil and butter until softened.
Add remaining vegetables. Cook for about 5 minutes.
Add stock. Bring to a boil.
Reduce heat. Simmer, covered, for about 1 hour until vegetables are soft.
Purée partially, leaving some pieces of vegetables for texture.
Stir in cream when ready to serve.
Reheat.
Garnish with chopped parsley.
Serves 8.

MUSHROOM & TARRAGON SOUP

1 pound mushrooms, chopped
4 cups chicken stock
1/4 cup fresh tarragon, lightly
    packed
Whipping cream

Finely chop tarragon.
Put mushrooms, chicken stock and 2 tablespoons of
tarragon in a pot.
Bring to a boil. Reduce heat. Simmer, covered, for about
10 minutes.
Add cream when ready to serve.
Reheat.
Sprinkle remaining tarragon on top as garnish.
Serves 4.

ZUCCHINI CURRY SOUP

4 zucchini, cut into thick slices
1 onion, chopped
1 T curry powder
3 cups chicken stock
Salt and pepper
Whipping cream or half and half
Chives, chopped

Put zucchini, onion, curry powder and stock in a saucepan. Bring to a boil.
Reduce heat. Simmer, covered, for about 30 minutes. Stir occasionally.
Purée mixture.
Add salt and pepper to taste.
When ready to serve, stir in cream.
Reheat. Garnish with chopped chives if desired.
Serves 6.

SPINACH SOUP

2 10 oz packages frozen spinach or
    comparable amount of
    fresh spinach
1 T lemon juice
3 T butter
3 T flour
2 cups milk
1/8 t nutmeg
Salt and pepper to taste
1/4 cup Romano cheese, freshly
    grated (optional)

Cook spinach according to package directions, or until tender, if fresh.
Put spinach and lemon juice in blender. Purée.
Melt butter in a large saucepan.
Stir in flour to make a smooth paste.
Add milk gradually, stirring constantly.
Cook until thickened.
Stir in nutmeg, spinach and cheese.
Cook until heated through.
Season with salt and pepper.
More milk may be added if a thinner soup is desired.
Serves 4 to 6.

LENTIL SOUP

1 14 1/2 ounce can tomatoes
4 cups water
1 cup lentils, rinsed
1 cup onion, diced
1 clove garlic, minced
2 T Worcestershire sauce
1 T lemon juice
2 T parsley, chopped
Salt and pepper

Combine all ingredients in a large pot.
Bring to a boil.
Reduce heat. Simmer with pot covered for 1 to 1 1/2
hours, or until lentils are cooked.
Serves 8.

CREAMY CABBAGE SOUP

1/4 cup butter
3 cups cabbage, finely shredded
3/4 cup chicken stock
1 1/4 cups milk or half and half
Salt and white pepper

Melt butter in a medium saucepan over low heat.
Add cabbage.
Cover. Cook about 30 minutes, or until cabbage is soft.
Stir occasionally.
Add stock to cooked cabbage.
Purée.
Return to saucepan. Bring to a boil. Reduce heat.
Add milk. Simmer until heated through.
Season with salt and pepper.
Serves 4.

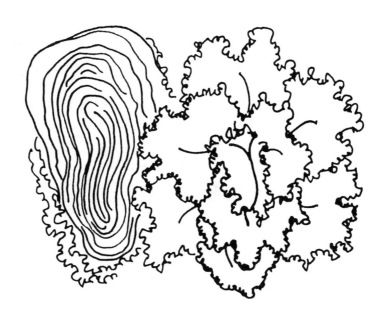

CARROT SOUP

1 1/2 pounds carrots, sliced
4 cups chicken stock
3/4 t curry powder
2 T lemon juice
Dash of cayenne pepper
Whipping cream or half and half

Put carrots into a large pot.
Add chicken stock and curry.
Simmer until carrots are soft.
Add lemon juice and cayenne pepper.
Purée.
Before serving, add cream to taste.
Reheat.
Serves 6.

GREEN PEA SOUP

1 large onion, finely chopped
1/4 cup butter
2 large potatoes, cubed
2 16 ounce packages frozen peas
2 t salt
1/2 t pepper
2 cups milk
1/2 cup half and half

Sauté onions in butter in a saucepan until tender, but not brown.
Add potatoes and 1 cup boiling water. Cover. Cook until potatoes are tender.
Meanwhile, combine peas 1 teaspoon salt and 1 cup boiling water in a saucepan. Cover. Cook over medium heat until peas are tender.
Place potato mixture and peas in blender.
Purée.
Pour mixture into large saucepan.
Stir in milk, remaining salt and pepper and half and half.
Place over low heat. Heat through, adding more half and half if too thick.
Serves 6.

POTATO & CELERY SOUP

2 T butter
1/2 bunch celery, cut into 1 inch
   pieces
2 medium onions, chopped
1 pound potatoes, peeled and
   quartered
2 1/2 cups chicken stock
Salt and pepper to taste
2/3 cup milk
1/2 to 3/4 cup Cheddar cheese,
   grated

Melt butter in saucepan. Add celery and onions. Cook
gently without browning.
Add potatoes and chicken stock.
Salt and pepper to taste.
Bring to a boil. Reduce heat. Simmer, covered, until
potatoes are tender.
Purée.
Add milk when ready to serve.
Reheat.
Sprinkle with cheese.
Serves 6.

QUICK CREAMY CHILE SOUP

1 can (4 ounce) green chiles
2 cans (10 1/2 ounces each) cream of
    mushroom soup
1 1/2 cups milk
1/2 cup sour cream

Blend all ingredients in blender until smooth. Heat very
slowly over low heat until hot, but not boiling.
Makes about 4 servings.

CURRIED MUSHROOM BARLEY SOUP

2 T butter
1 cup sliced carrots
1 cup chopped onion
1 pound mushrooms, sliced
4 t curry powder
2 (13 3/4 ounce) cans chicken broth
1 (14 1/2 ounce) can stewed tomatoes
1/2 cup quick-cooking barley

In a large saucepan melt butter. Add carrots and onion.
Cook, stirring occasionally until carrots are crisp-tender,
about 5 minutes. Add mushrooms. Cook, stirring
frequently until mushrooms are tender, about 5 minutes.
Add curry powder, stirring constantly about 1 minute.
Stir in chicken broth, tomatoes and barley.
Bring to a boil. Reduce heat and simmer covered, until
barley is tender
(about 20 minutes).

SALADS

DILLED CUCUMBERS
&
SOUR CREAM

2 cucumbers
1 cup sour cream
2 t onion, minced
2 T lemon juice
1 T wine vinegar
1/2 t dillseed
1 t salt
Lettuce leaves

Peel cucumbers. Slice paper thin.
Place in a bowl. Chill well.
Place sour cream, onion, lemon juice, vinegar, dillseed,
and salt in a medium bowl.
Blend thoroughly.
Add cucumbers.
Toss lightly until coated.
Line a salad bowl with lettuce.
Add cucumber mixture.
Serves 4.

CURRIED CHICKEN SALAD

3 cups chicken breast, cooked and
 diced
1 1/2 cups celery, thinly sliced
1 cup seedless green grapes
1 T lemon juice
1 t salt
1/4 t pepper

Curry mayonnaise:
1 cup oil
1 T vinegar
1 egg
1/2 t salt
1/8 t paprika
1/4 t dry mustard
Dash of cayenne pepper
1 1/2 t curry powder

Curry mayonnaise
Pour 1/4 cup of oil in blender.
Add remaining ingredients.
Blend for 5 seconds, then slowly add the remaining oil.

Combine chicken with celery, grapes, lemon juice,
pepper, salt, and curry mayonnaise.
Toss lightly until just blended.
Chill about 2 hours.
To serve, place on a bed of lettuce.
Serves 6.

SALAD NICOISE

A classic salad, combining seasonal salad ingredients with tuna, egg and a zesty dressing.

Serve with Honey Mustard Scones for a special lunch.

5 eggs, hard cooked
1 head green leaf lettuce
2 pounds small red potatoes
    unpeeled, cooked and sliced
1/2 pound green beans, cooked
1 12 ounce can tuna,drained and flaked
2 medium tomatoes, cut into wedges
12 olives
Anchovy fillets, for garnish, if desired

Halve 3 eggs. Set aside.
Separate yolks from whites of remaining two eggs for use in dressing. Chop whites. Set aside for garnish.

Salad Nicoise Dressing:

> 1/2 cup mayonnaise
> 1/3 cup Dijon mustard
> 1/4 cup milk
> 2 T chives, chopped
> 1 t sugar

In bowl, mash egg yolks, reserved as indicated above.
Stir in mayonnaise, mustard, milk, chives, and sugar until
smooth.

Line individual serving plates with lettuce leaves.
Arrange potatoes, green beans, tuna, tomatoes, halved
eggs and olives on lettuce.
Garnish with chopped egg whites and anchovies.
Serve with dressing.
Serves 6.

ENGLISH ROSE CLASSIC SALAD

1 head green leaf lettuce
1 cucumber, peeled and thinly sliced
1/2 red onion, peeled and thinly
sliced
1 cup red cabbage, thinly sliced
2 tomatoes, cut into small wedges
Garlic croutons
English Rose Creamy Vinaigrette
Dressing

Tear lettuce into small pieces. Put in salad bowl.
Add cucumber, onion, cabbage, tomatoes and croutons.
Serve with *English Rose Restaurant Creamy Vinaigrette*
Special Dressing .
Serves 4

English Rose Restaurant Creamy Vinaigrette
Special Dressing

>
> 1/2 medium onion
> 1/2 t garlic powder
> 1 1/2 t sugar
> 1/2 t salt
> 1/4 t dry mustard
> 1/8 t pepper
> 1 cup oil
> 1/2 cup cider vinegar
> 2 t commercial salad seasoning

Place all ingredients in blender.
Blend at high speed for 1 minute.
Keep refrigerated.

SAVORY WATERCRESS & MUSHROOM SALAD with POPPY SEED DRESSING

8 mushrooms, sliced thinly
1/2 red onion, sliced thinly and separated into rings
1 large bunch watercress, tough stems removed

Arrange mushrooms and onion rings on bed of watercress.
Top with dressing.

Poppy seed dressing:

1/4 cup honey
1/4 cup lemon juice
3/4 cup walnut or safflower oil
1 T Dijon style mustard
1 green onion, minced
1 T poppy seeds
1/2 t salt

Thoroughly combine all ingredients.

DILL-ARTICHOKE POTATO SALAD

3 pounds whole tiny new potatoes
   or unpeeled white potatoes cut
   into small pieces
1 cup mayonnaise
2 T red wine vinegar
2 T Dijon mustard
1 T lemon-pepper seasoning
1 T snipped fresh dill *or*
   2 to 3 t dried
4 hard cooked eggs, peeled and
   chopped
2 6 ounce jars marinated artichoke
   hearts, drained and sliced
3/4 cup chopped onion
2 T chopped dill pickle

Scrub potatoes. Cook in a covered saucepan for approximately 20 minutes, or until just tender. Drain and cool. Cut into bite sized pieces.

In very large bowl stir together mayonnaise, vinegar, mustard, lemon-pepper seasoning, and dill. Gently fold in cooked potatoes, eggs, artichoke hearts, onion and pickle. Cover and chill 4 to 24 hours. Stir gently before serving.
Serves 16.

SPINACH SALAD
with
FETA & APPLE

3/4 pound fresh spinach, washed, trimmed and torn

2 tart green apples, cut into 1 inch cubes (unpeeled)

3 T rice wine vinegar, additional

2 T olive oil

1/4 cup orange juice

1 1/2 T honey

1 t Dijon mustard

3/4 cup feta cheese, crumbled

Place spinach in large salad bowl. Toss apples with 1 tablespoon of the vinegar. Process the next four ingredients, plus remaining 2 tablespoons vinegar, in a blender. Pour over spinach, tossing well. Sprinkle with the apples and cheese. Serve immediately.
Serves 8.

LIGHT
LUNCHES

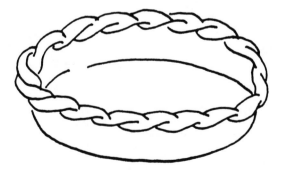

STILTON CHEESE
&
HERB PATE

5 ounces Stilton cheese
5 ounces Cheddar cheese
5 T whipping cream
1 t mixed herbs
1 t garlic salt

Grate cheese finely. Add herbs and garlic salt. Add cream. Mix to the consistency of a soft paste.
Serve paté, garnished with a lettuce leaf and sprinkled with paprika, with thinly sliced hot toast.
Serves 4.

SALMON PATE

1 15 ounce can red salmon
8 ounces cream cheese, softened
1 clove garlic, pressed
1/2 cup small curd cottage cheese
1/4 cup onion, minced
1 t fines herbes
1/2 t thyme
1 cup parsley, chopped
1/2 cup walnuts or pecans, chopped

Drain salmon. Remove any skin and bones.
Combine cream cheese, garlic, cottage cheese, onion and
seasonings until well blended.
Stir in salmon.
Chill for 3 hours. Mixture will be soft. Roll in parsley
and chopped nuts.
Serve with crackers or with a salad and French bread.
Serves 4.

BUCK RAREBIT

6 eggs
2 cups Cheddar cheese, grated
1 t Worcestershire sauce
Pepper
4 slices bread

Beat 2 of the eggs well. Mix in cheese, Worcestershire
sauce, and pepper to taste.
Toast bread lightly on both sides. Spread cheese mixture
on each slice.
Put under a broiler until cheese melts and browns.
Meanwhile, poach the remaining eggs and serve one on
each toasted cheese slice.
Serves 4.

SCOTCH EGGS

6 eggs, hard cooked
1 pound pork sausage meat
1 egg
4 t cold water
1 cup fresh soft bread crumbs
Flour
Oil

Dust eggs with flour.
Divide sausage meat into 6 portions.
Wrap each egg completely in a portion of sausage meat.
Beat egg with water.
Dip sausage meat in egg mixture.
Coat with bread crumbs.
Fry in hot oil for 8 to 10 minutes. Drain on paper towels.
Serve with salad.
Serves 3.

QUICHE

1 10 inch pastry shell, unbaked
1/4 cup onion, chopped
1/2 cup mushrooms, chopped
2/3 cup Swiss cheese, grated
6 eggs, beaten well
1/2 t salt
1/2 t pepper
1 1/3 cups whipping cream

Your choice of additional fillings might include cooked bacon bits, chopped asparagus, chopped broccoli, chopped tomatoes, cooked chopped spinach (squeezed to eliminate moisture), shrimp, ham, sausage, or any combination of these.

Preheat oven to 350 degrees.

Arrange onions and mushrooms in bottom of pastry shell.
Spread any other vegetable or meat you might choose.
Top with grated cheese.
In a mixing bowl, mix eggs well with cream and salt and pepper. Pour into pastry shell.
Bake for about 1 hour, or until quiche is lightly browned and set in the middle.
Turn quiche halfway through baking so it cooks evenly.
Serves 6.

SALMON QUICHE

1 7 1/2 ounce red salmon, drained
1/4 cup olives, sliced
2 T parsley, chopped
1/2 cup Cheddar cheese, grated
5 eggs, beaten
1 1/3 cups whipping cream
1/4 t salt
1/2 t onion powder
1 10 inch pastry shell, unbaked

Preheat oven to 350 degrees.

Remove any skin and bones from salmon.
In a small bowl, lightly mix the salmon with olives,
parsley, and cheese.
In a separate bowl, combine eggs with cream, salt, and
onion powder.
Spread salmon mixture in pastry shell.
Pour egg mixture over all.
Bake approximately 1 hour, or until set.
Serves 6.

ENGLISH-STYLE SANDWICHES

Thinly sliced bread, buttered
Choice of fillings

Cream Cheese and Cucumber

Spread one side of bread with softened cream cheese.
Top with peeled and thinly sliced cucumbers.
Sprinkle with malt vinegar and salt and pepper to taste.
Top with second slice of bread.

Salmon and Cucumber

Drain and flake canned red salmon.
Spread on one side of bread. Top with thinly sliced
cucumbers.
Sprinkle with malt vinegar and salt and pepper to taste.
Top with second slice of bread.

Cheese and Chutney

Cover one side of bread with slice of Cheddar cheese or
other cheese of your choice.
Spread with chutney.
Top with second slice of bread.

Watercress

Wash watercress well, and dry. Arrange on one side of bread.
Sprinkle with malt vinegar and salt and pepper to taste.
Top with second slice of bread.

Ham

Slice ham very thinly.
Arrange on one side of bread.
Spread a little hot English mustard on other piece of bread if desired.
Top with second slice of bread.

Cut sandwiches on diagonal, and again into quarters if desired.

TOAD-in-the-HOLE

A simple, but hearty dish of English sausages baked in Yorkshire Pudding batter.

8 English sausages (Bangers)
Yorkshire Pudding batter

Preheat oven to 400 degrees.

Prepare Yorkshire Pudding batter according to recipe. Refrigerate for at least 1 hour.
Place sausages side by side in heavy skillet. Prick them once or twice with fork.
Sprinkle with 2 tablespoons water.
Cover pan tightly. Cook over low heat for 3 minutes.
Remove cover. Increase heat to moderate. Continue to cook, turning frequently, until water has evaporated and sausages have browned in their own fat.
Arrange sausages in single layer in 10 x 15x 21/2 inch baking dish. Keep the sausages at least one inch apart.
Pour batter over sausages.
Bake for 15 minutes.
Reduce heat to 375 degrees. Bake for 15 minutes longer, or until pudding has risen over top of pan and is crisp and brown.
Serve at once, with a brown gravy and vegetable of your choice.
Serves 4.

PLOUGHMAN'S LUNCH

A hearty but simple meal, traditionally enjoyed by the farmers in the fields. Now served in most pubs throughout England, accompanied by a glass of ale.

1 apple, sliced and cored
Freshly baked bread or French bread
Cheddar cheese, or any other cheeses of
your choice, sliced
Pickled onions
Chutney

Arrange the above on a serving plate.
Enjoy with a glass of ale.
Serves 1.

MIXED VEGETABLE CURRY

1 small cauliflower, cut into flowerets
1 1/3 cups carrots, diced
1 1/4 cups potatoes, diced
1 cup water
1 1/2 cups green peas
3 T butter or margarine
1 large onion, sliced
1 T curry powder
1 T flour
Salt to taste
2 T mango chutney
Water or chicken stock as needed
2/3 cup half and half
2 T blanched almonds
4 eggs, hard cooked and cut in wedges
Paprika

Steam cauliflower, carrots and potatoes 6 minutes, or
until tender.
Bring water to boil in medium saucepan. Add peas .
Cook 5 minutes.
Drain vegetables, reserving cooking liquid from peas.
Keep vegetables warm.
Melt butter in large saucepan.
Add onion. Sauté over low heat 5 minutes.
Stir in curry powder, flour, and salt. Cook 1 minute.

Stir in chutney.

Pour cooking liquid into 2 cup measuring cup. Add enough water or chicken stock to make 2 cups.

Gradually stir into curry mixture. Bring to a boil.

Simmer 5 minutes.

Stir in half and half. Stir in vegetables.

Heat until hot. Stir in almonds.

Serve hot, garnished with egg wedges and paprika.

Serve with hot rice.

Serves 4.

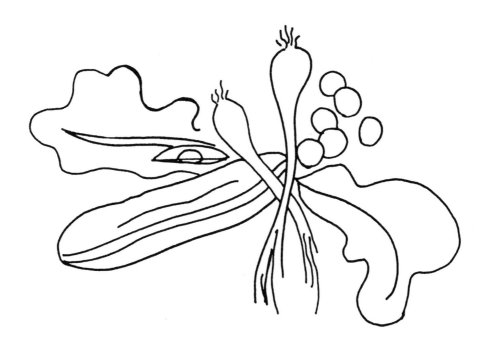

BANGER & ONION SANDWICH

1 English Banger (sausage)
1 slice onion
1 crusty French roll, or French bread
 cut to size of sausage
Mustard

Cook banger either by grilling, frying or broiling.
Cut in half lengthwise.
Meanwhile, fry onion in a little oil until it starts to brown.
Place cooked banger and cooked onion slice on roll or
French bread.
Spread on mustard.
Makes 1 sandwich.

SHRIMP CAKES

Cakes
1/2 pound raw shrimp
1 shallot, peeled and finely chopped
1/4 cup finely chopped red pepper
1/4 t dried crushed tarragon
1 T mayonnaise
1 egg white
1/4 cup bread crumbs
salt
white pepper
1 T butter
lemon wedges for garnish

Sauce
1 T cocktail sauce
2 T mayonnaise
1 T capers

Chop shrimp finely. Place in small mixing bowl along with shallot, bell pepper, tarragon, mayonnaise, egg white, and bread crumbs. Salt and pepper to taste. Mix well. Form into 4 cakes.

Melt butter in medium skillet. Fry cakes over medium heat until golden, about 5 minutes per side.

Meanwhile, stir together cocktail sauce, mayonnaise and capers for sauce. Garnish with lemon wedges. Serve sauce on the side.

EASY EGGLESS
SPINACH SOUFFLE

2 packages chopped frozen spinach
1 16 ounce carton sour cream
1 envelope onion soup mix
1 can french-fried onion rings

Mix sour cream and soup mix together. Stir in spinach.
Place in buttered 2 quart shallow baking dish. Sprinkle
onion rings on top. Bake at 350° for about 20-25 minutes.
Serves 8

CONDIMENTS

APPLE CHUTNEY

5 pounds apples
1 T salt
1 T ground ginger
6 chile peppers, chopped
2 cups brown sugar
1 1/4 to 2 1/2 cups vinegar
1/2 pound onions, minced
1 1/4 cups pitted dates, chopped
1 1/3 cups raisins

Peel and slice apples.

Put salt, ginger, peppers, and sugar into a pan with some of the vinegar.

Add apples and onions.

Bring to a boil.

Add chopped dates and raisins. Simmer until thick and brown, adding more vinegar as required. The apples make a lot of juice, but the chutney should not be runny.

Put into warm jars. Cover well.

Refrigerate.

CRANBERRY &
RAISIN CHUTNEY

1 pound marmalade
1 15 ounce can whole berry
   cranberry sauce, or freshly
   made cranberry sauce
1/2 cup vinegar
1 cup raisins
1 large onion, chopped
1 orange, unpeeled and chopped
1 large garlic clove, minced
1/4 t mace
1/4 t ground ginger
1/4 t allspice
1/4 t cinnamon
1 t red pepper flakes

Put all ingredients in a microwave-safe bowl. Mix well.
Cook in microwave at high speed for 40 minutes, or until
thickened.
Stir mixture at 10 minute intervals.
Remove from microwave. Let cool before putting into
jars.
Refrigerate.

RHUBARB CHUTNEY

2 pounds rhubarb
1/2 pound onions, finely chopped
3 cups brown sugar
1 1/3 cups seedless white raisins
1 1/2 T mustard seeds
1 t allspice
1 t pepper
1 t ground ginger
1 t salt
1/4 t cayenne pepper
2 1/2 cups vinegar

Cut rhubarb into 1 inch lengths.
Put all ingredients into a heavy pan. Simmer gently,
stirring frequently until mixture is consistency of jam.
Put into jars. Cover tightly.
Refrigerate.

PICKLED ONIONS

            2 pounds boiling onions
            5 cups vinegar
            2 t allspice
            1 t pickling spice
            2 t peppercorns
            6 t sugar

Peel onions. Place in a clean, dry jar.
Boil vinegar with spices and sugar. Let cool.
When cold, pour vinegar mixture over onions, filling the
jar completely.
Cover and store in a dry place. The pickled onions will be
ready in 2 weeks.

HORSERADISH SAUCE

Excellent served as accompaniment to roast beef or fish.
Especially tasty as an accent to grilled salmon.

1/4 cup bottled horseradish,
   drained
1 T white wine vinegar
1 t sugar
1/4 t dry English mustard
1/2 t salt
1/2 t white pepper
1/2 cup whipping cream, chilled

In small bowl, stir horseradish, vinegar, sugar, mustard,
salt, and pepper together until well blended.
Beat cream until stiff peaks form.
Pour horseradish mixture over cream.
With a rubber spatula, fold together lightly, but
thoroughly.
Makes 1 cup.

MOCK CLOTTED CREAM

A heavy cream to spread on top of scones, instead of butter, along with jam.

1 cube unsalted butter, frozen
1/2 pint whipping cream

In small bowl, whip cream until soft peaks form.
Into another small bowl, grate frozen butter.
With spoon, fold grated butter into whipped cream.
Keep refrigerated until served.
Makes about 2 cups.

To make smaller quantities, grated butter may be refrozen and added to whipped cream as needed.

ORANGE MARMALADE

1 orange, thinly sliced
1 lemon, thinly sliced
1 grapefruit, thinly sliced
Water, as needed
Sugar, as needed

For each cup of fruit, add 3 cups water.
Let stand overnight in glass bowl.
Boil fruit rapidly until tender.
Add one cup sugar for each cup fruit and liquid mixture.
Continue boiling until fruit is clear. Syrup should sheet from spoon.
Remove from stove top.
Allow to stand for 5 minutes. Stir often to prevent fruit from floating.
Pour into sterilized jars. Fill to 1/4 inch of top.
Cover with paraffin.
Makes six 8 ounce jars.

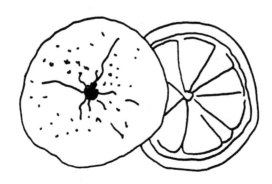

LEMON CURD

6 lemons
3/4 cup butter
2 2/3 cups sugar
6 eggs, well beaten

In double boiler, melt butter with sugar.

Meanwhile, peel and juice lemons. Put rind and juice in blender.

Mix at high speed until the rind is in very small pieces. If using a food processor, cut lemons and put in processor. Pulse until rind is in very small pieces.

Add to the butter and sugar.

When butter and sugar mixture is melted, add eggs, stirring constantly until eggs are completely mixed in.

Continue cooking for about 1 hour, or until mixture thickens. Stir often.

Be sure not to let the water boil dry in the double boiler.

When cooled, put into jars.

Refrigerate.

The curd will thicken more when it is chilled.

Lemon curd will keep for several months in the refrigerator.

RASPBERRY JAM

The rule is jam tomorrow and jam yesterday, but never jam today. **—Alice in Wonderland**

    6 cups raspberries, well packed
    4 cups sugar
    1/3 cup lemon juice.

Combine berries and sugar in heavy saucepan.
Let stand until sugar dissolves. Stir often.
Place over high heat. Bring to rapid boil.
Boil 5 minutes, timing from minute mixture breaks into rolling boil.
Add lemon juice.
Boil 5 minutes more. Pour into sterilized jars. Seal with paraffin.
This jam is superb with scones.
Makes six 8 ounce jars.

MAIN DISHES

JULIE'S CREAMY BAKED CHICKEN

8 chicken breasts, boned
1 can cream of chicken soup or white sauce
1/2 cup dry white wine
1/2 pound Swiss cheese, thinly sliced
2 cups seasoned stuffing mix
1/3 cup melted butter

Preheat oven to 350 degrees.

Remove skin from chicken.
Arrange in large shallow pan.
Place a slice of Swiss cheese on each piece of chicken.
Stir together soup and wine or substitute white sauce for soup.

Mix well. Spoon evenly over chicken and cheese.
Crush stuffing mix. Sprinkle over top of chicken.
Evenly drizzle butter over all.
Bake uncovered at 350 degrees for about 1 hour, or until chicken is tender and stuffing is brown.
Serves 8.

White sauce

4 T butter
4 T flour
1/4 t salt
Dash white pepper
2 cups chicken stock

Melt butter. Blend in flour, salt and pepper.
Gradually add chicken stock, stirring constantly, until
mixture thickens.
Makes 2 cups.

CHICKEN FLAN

1 9 inch pie shell, unbaked
1 T butter
6 large mushrooms, chopped
1/4 cup ham, chopped
1/2 t salt
1/4 t white pepper
1/4 t cayenne pepper
2 T whipping cream or half and
    half
1 1/2 cups cooked chicken, cubed
3/4 cups Cheddar cheese, grated

Preheat oven to 400 degrees.

Place pie shell on a baking sheet.
In a small frying pan, melt butter over moderate heat.
When foam subsides, add mushrooms and cook for 3
minutes.
Stir in ham, salt, pepper, and cayenne pepper.
Remove from heat.
Stir in cream.
Spoon mixture over bottom of pie shell.
Lay chicken pieces on top. Sprinkle with cheese.
Bake for 20 to 30 minutes, or until the top is brown and
bubbling and pastry is lightly browned.
Serves 4 to 6.

SPICED CHICKEN with HONEY

1/4 cup butter
1/2 cup honey
4 T spiced mustard
1 t salt
1 t curry powder
3 pound roasting chicken, cut into 8
   pieces or
6 chicken breasts

Preheat oven to 375 degrees.

In a roasting pan, melt butter over medium heat.
When foam subsides, add honey, mustard, salt, and curry
powder.
Stir to mix well.
Remove from heat.
Add chicken pieces. Roll in mixture to coat thoroughly.
Arrange in one layer over bottom of tin.
Bake for 1 hour, or until tender. Baste frequently with
honey mixture.
Serve with cooking liquid poured over.
Serves 6.

BEEF & EGGPLANT CASSEROLE

                3 small eggplants
                1 T plus 1 t salt
                4 T vegetable oil
                2 pounds ground beef
                4 green onions, chopped
                6 tomatoes, chopped
                1 large green pepper, chopped
                1/4 t pepper
                1/2 t marjoram
                1 1/2 cups cheddar cheese, grated

Preheat oven to 350 degrees.

Cut eggplant into thin slices.
Place in a colander.
Sprinkle with 1 T salt.
Set aside for 30 minutes.
Meanwhile, in a large frying pan, brown beef, stirring
constantly, for about 5 minutes.
Add onions, tomatoes, and green pepper.
Cook for 5 more minutes, stirring occasionally.
Stir in remaining teaspoon of salt, pepper, and marjoram.
Reduce heat.
Simmer, stirring occasionally, for 15 minutes.

Remove from heat. Set aside.

Dry eggplant slices on paper towels.

In a large frying pan, heat oil over medium heat.

Add some of eggplant slices.

Fry for 2 to 3 minutes on each side, or until soft.

Repeat the process until all eggplant is cooked, adding more oil if necessary.

Place one third of eggplant in large oven-proof dish.

Cover with half the meat mixture, then with another third of eggplant.

Top with remaining meat and eggplant.

Sprinkle with cheese.

Bake 30 minutes, or until top is golden.

Serves 6.

CIDERED PORK, CHEESE, &
APPLE CASSEROLE

1 1/2 pounds pork tenderloin, cubed
2 cups onions, sliced
2 large cooking apples
1   cup dry cider or 1/2 cup apple
    cider and 1/2 cup beer
1 1/2 cups cheddar cheese, grated
1/4 t nutmeg
1/2 t salt
1/2 t pepper

Preheat oven to 350 degrees.

Peel, core, and slice apples.
Brown pork quickly, with onion, in a little hot oil.
Put meat and onion in a casserole.
Sprinkle flour over juices left in frying pan.
Gradually add cider and seasonings.
Stir until thickened.
Pour over meat and onions in casserole.
Cover with apples.
Bake covered 1 hour.
Sprinkle with cheese.
Increase oven temperature to 400 degrees.
Bake uncovered for half an hour.
Serves 4.

PORK CHOPS in GINGER ALE

4 pork chops
a little brown sugar
2 onions, chopped
1 T tomato paste
4 T butter
1 T flour
1 1/3 cups ginger ale
Salt and pepper to taste

Preheat oven to 350 degrees.

Sauté onions in half the butter until golden brown.
Place in a casserole dish.
Brown chops on both sides in rest of butter.
Place on top of onions.
Sprinkle with brown sugar.
Mix tomato paste and flour. Add ginger ale.
Pour over chops.
Season with salt and pepper.
Bake for about one hour, until chops are tender.
Serves 4.

GLAMORGAN SAUSAGES

Made from a tasty mixture of cheese, onion, and herbs

1 large onion, finely chopped
3/4 cup Cheddar cheese, grated
1 cup fresh white bread crumbs
1 T parsley, chopped
1/2 t dried thyme
1 t salt
1/2 t black pepper
1/4 t dry mustard
1 egg , separated
2 T flour
1 cup dry white bread crumbs
1/4 cup butter
2 T vegetable oil

In a mixing bowl, combine onion, cheese, fresh bread crumbs, parsley, thyme, salt, pepper, mustard, and egg yolk.
Lightly beat egg white in separate bowl. Set aside.
With your hands, shape mixture into 8 sausages.
Dip in flour, then in lightly beaten egg whites.
Roll in dry bread crumbs.
In a large frying pan, melt butter and oil over medium heat.
When foam subsides, add sausages.
Fry, turning occasionally, for 5 to 8 minutes, or until well browned on all sides.
Serves 2.

YORKSHIRE PANCAKES

Crunchy pancakes with onion and beef.

4 eggs, separated
1/2 pound ground beef
1/2 t salt
1/2 t pepper
1/2 t baking powder
1 small onion, finely chopped
1 T Worcestershire sauce
2 T parsley, chopped
1/2 t dried basil
3 T vegetable oil

In a large bowl, beat egg yolks until thick.
Fold in beef, salt, pepper, baking powder, onion,
Worcestershire sauce, parsley, and basil.
Stir until ingredients are combined.
Beat egg whites until they form stiff peaks. Using a metal
spoon, gently fold them into beef mixture.
In large frying pan, heat oil over moderate heat.
Drop tablespoons of beef mixture into hot oil.
Fry for 3 minutes, or until pancakes are puffed up and
brown at the edges.
Turn and fry for another 2 to 3 minutes.
Drain on paper towels.
Keep warm while you fry remaining beef mixture.
Serve as a main course with vegetables.
Serves 4 to 6.

CORNISH PASTIES

These individual meat pies were traditionally eaten by the Cornish tin miners for their lunch. The pasty was marked at one end with the miner's initials, so that if part of it was uneaten it could be claimed later by its owner.

Filling

2 pounds ground chuck
1 large potato, peeled and cubed
1 large onion, chopped
1 turnip, peeled and chopped
1 10 ounce package frozen peas and carrots or comparable quantity fresh vegetables
1 t salt
1 t pepper

Pastry

1 1/3 pounds flour
2/3 pounds shortening
Cold water
1 egg, beaten

Preheat oven to 375 degrees.

Mix together in a large bowl all ingredients for filling.

In another bowl mix flour with shortening until it resembles coarse bread crumbs. Use either your hands or pastry cutter.

With a wooden spoon, stir in cold water a little at a time until a firm dough is formed.

Roll out pastry on floured board into 8 six inch circles, using a large pastry cutter or a small plate. The scraps can be worked together and rolled out again until you have enough circles.

Divide filling into 8 portions.

Place an oblong mound of filling in center of each pastry circle.

Moisten edges of pastry with water.

Bring two sides together, pressing firmly to seal.

Place on greased cookie sheet.

Brush with egg.

Bake for about an hour, or until golden brown.

Serve warm with salad and chutney.

Serves 8.

These freeze very well.

SHEPHERD'S PIE

1 medium onion, chopped
1 pound ground chuck
1 10 ounce package frozen peas and carrots or comparable amount fresh vegetables
3 T Worcestershire sauce
5 T H.P. Steak Sauce or other English-style sauce
3 t Bisto gravy powder
3/4 cup water
1 t salt
1/2 t pepper
2 large potatoes, cooked and mashed
1/4 cup Cheddar cheese, grated

Preheat oven to 375 degrees.

In large saucepan, brown beef with chopped onions until meat is crumbly.
Mix Bisto powder with water. Add to meat mixture.
Add remaining ingredients, except potatoes and cheese.
Simmer on low heat, stirring occasionally, for about 20 minutes, until gravy thickens.
Put into four individual ramekins, or into one ovenproof casserole. Top with mashed potatoes. Draw decorative lines on top with fork. Sprinkle with cheese.
Bake for about 45 minutes, until potatoes start to brown.
Serves 4.

CHICKEN CURRY

6 boneless chicken breasts
3 stalks celery, diced
2 medium green apples, peeled and
   diced
1 medium onion, diced
3 cups water
1 package S&B golden (medium)
   curry powder
3 T orange marmalade
3 T steak sauce
3/4 cup raisins
1/2 cube butter

Poach chicken until cooked through. Remove to bowl.
Cool in refrigerator until cool enough to handle.
Reserve the poaching liquid. Cut chicken into small pieces.
Melt butter in a large saucepan. Add cut up onions, apples
and celery. Sauté for about 5 minutes. Add chicken, water,
raisins, curry paste, marmalade, and steak sauce.
Cook, stirring occasionally, at low heat for about 15
minutes.
Serve over rice.
Makes 6 servings.

ROAST BEEF

Served with Yorkshire Pudding, this is a traditional English feast.

8 pound standing rib roast

Preheat oven to 450 degrees.

Place beef, fat side up, in a large shallow roasting pan. Roast for 20 minutes.
Reduce heat to 325 degrees. Continue to roast, without basting, for about 90 minutes, or until cooked to your taste.
Estimate 12 minutes per pound for rare beef, 15 minutes per pound for medium, and 20 minutes per pound for well.
Transfer beef to heated platter.
If you plan to serve beef with Yorkshire Pudding, increase oven to 400 degrees as soon as beef is cooked.
Drape foil loosely over roast while pudding bakes.
Slice beef thinly just before serving.
Serve with horseradish sauce if desired.
Serves 6 to 8.

YORKSHIRE PUDDING

2 eggs
1/2 t salt
1 cup flour
1 cup milk
2 T roast beef drippings or 2 T lard

Preheat oven to 400 degrees.

In blender jar combine eggs, salt, flour, and milk. Blend at high speed for 2 to 3 seconds. Turn off machine, scrape down sides of jar, and blend again for 40 seconds.
To make by hand, beat eggs and salt with whisk or electric beater until frothy. Slowly add flour, beating constantly. Pour in milk in thin stream. Beat until mixture is smooth and creamy.
Refrigerate for at least 1 hour.
In a 10x15x 2 1/2 inch roasting pan, heat drippings until they splutter, either on the stove or in the oven.
Briefly beat batter again.
Pour into pan.
Bake in middle of oven for 15 minutes.
Reduce heat to 375 degrees. Bake an additional 15 minutes, or until pudding has risen over top of pan and is crisp and brown.
With a sharp knife, divide into portions. Serve immediately.
Serves 6 to 8.

HOT POT

A traditional English dish. A stew with layers of beef, carrots, onions and potatoes.

>   2 pounds top round of beef,
>   trimmed and cut into large cubes
>   1 t salt
>   1/4 t pepper
>   3/4 pound carrots, thickly sliced
>   2 large onions, thickly sliced
>   1 1/2 pounds potatoes, peeled and
>   thickly sliced
>   2 1/2 cups beef stock

Preheat oven to 325 degrees.

Arrange a layer of beef in an oven proof casserole.
Sprinkle with a little of the salt and pepper.
Top with layer of carrots, onions, and potatoes.
Continue making layers until all ingredients have been used, ending with a layer of potatoes, arranged in overlapping slices.
Pour in stock.
Cover. Bake for 2 to 2 1/2 hours, or until the meat is tender.
Increase oven temperature to 400 degrees.
Remove lid. Cook for an additional 30 minutes, or until potatoes are browned on top.
Serves 4.

FISH CAKES

10 ounce white fish filets, cooked
    and flaked or red salmon cooked
    or canned
1/2 pound potatoes, cooked and
    mashed
1 T butter
1 egg
1 T flour
1/2 t salt
1/4 t cayenne pepper
2 T parsley, chopped
1 egg, lightly beaten
1 1/2 cups fine dry bread crumbs
4 T vegetable oil

In large mixing bowl, combine fish, potatoes, butter, egg,
flour, salt, cayenne pepper, and parsley.
Mix well with wooden spoon.
Place in refrigerator to chill for 1 hour.
With floured hands, shape mixture into 6 balls.
On a lightly floured board, flatten balls into patties.
Dip patties in beaten egg.
Roll in bread crumbs to coat thoroughly.
In a large heavy frying pan, heat oil over high heat.
Add fish cakes.
Fry for 5 to 8 minutes, turning frequently until golden
brown on all sides.
Serves 2.

FISH with PARSLEY SAUCE

1 1/2 pounds white fish filets, skinned
1 large onion, sliced thinly and separated into rings
2 cups milk
1/4 t salt
2 T butter
2 T flour
1/4 t white pepper
4 T parsley, chopped

Cut fish into serving pieces. Place on bottom of heavy saucepan.

Top with onion rings.

Pour milk over fish. Sprinkle with salt.

Cook over moderate heat to just below boiling point.

Reduce heat. Simmer for 15 minutes.

Remove fish and onions.

Place in a warmed serving dish. Keep warm.

Set cooking liquid aside.

In a small saucepan, melt butter over moderate heat.

Stir in flour to make a smooth paste.

Gradually add reserved liquid, stirring constantly.

Cook for 2 to 3 minutes, or until thick and smooth.

Stir in pepper and parsley.

Reduce heat. Cook for an additional minute.

Pour sauce over fish.

Serves 4.

FISH & POTATO PIE

2 pounds white fish fillets, skinned
  and cut into small chunks
4 potatoes, cooked and sliced
1/2 cup milk
2 eggs
1 t salt
1/4 t white pepper
3 tomatoes, sliced
2/3 cup fine dry breadcrumbs
1/2 cup Cheddar cheese, grated
2 T butter

Preheat oven to 350 degrees.

Arrange fish and potatoes in layers in medium sized
baking dish, finishing with potato.
Beat milk and eggs together.
Add salt and pepper. Pour over fish and potatoes.
Arrange tomato slices on top.
Combine breadcrumbs and cheese. Sprinkle over tomato
slices.
Dot with butter.
Bake for 50 to 60 minutes, or until top is brown and crisp.
Serves 6.

SHRIMP CURRY

5 T butter
6 T flour
2 t curry powder
1 1/4 t salt
1 1/2 t sugar
1/4 t ginger
2 cups milk
1 cup chicken boullion
1/2 cup onion, minced
2 cups cooked shrimp
1 t lemon juice
1 10 ounce package frozen peas
and carrots or comparable fresh
vegetables.

Sauté onion.
Melt butter in medium saucepan.
Stir in flour, curry, salt, sugar, and ginger.
Gradually stir in boullion and milk, stirring constantly.
When thickened, add onions, shrimp, lemon juice, and
peas and carrots.
Cook another 5 minutes, stirring constantly.
Serve over rice or puff pastry shells.
Serves 6.

FISH GRILLED with CHEESE

4 white fish fillets
2 T butter
1 small onion, minced
1 cup Cheddar cheese, grated
1 t mustard
2 t ketchup
1/2 t salt
1/4 t pepper
1/8 t cayenne pepper

Preheat broiler to high.

Place fish on a broiler pan. Dot with butter.
Reduce heat to moderate. Broil for 5 to 6 minutes on each side, or until fish flakes easily.
Meanwhile, combine remaining ingredients.
Mash well with wooden spoon.
Remove fish from heat.
Spread some of mixture on top of each fillet.
Return to heat. Cook for an additional 3 to 5 minutes, or until cheese mixture is bubbling and beginning to brown.
Serves 4.

INDIVIDUAL BEEF WELLINGTONS

4 beef tenderloin steaks, cut 1 inch thick
4 patty shells. If using frozen patty
    shells, thaw.
1/4 cup liver spread
1 egg, beaten
3 t cornstarch
2 t instant beef bouillon granules
1/2 t dried basil
4 T dry red wine

Preheat oven to 425 degrees.
Brush steaks with cooking oil.
Sprinkle with a litle salt and pepper.
In hot skillet, quickly brown 2 minutes on each side.
Cool at least 15 minutes.
Roll each patty shell into an 8 inch circle.
Spread liver over circles to within 1 inch of edge.
Center one steak atop each circle.
Brush edge of pastry with a little beaten egg.
Bring edges together to wrap meat. Press edges to seal.
Place seam side down in greased shallow baking pan.
Make small slash in top of each. Brush egg over pastry.
Bake about 20 minutes for medium doneness.
Meanwhile, combine cornstarch, bouillon granules, basil and 1 cup water.
Cook and stir for about 2 minutes until thickened and bubbly.
Stir in wine. Heat through. Serve with beef.
Serves 4.

CHICKEN FLORENTINE

1 sheet frozen puff pastry, thawed for
   20 minutes
4 chicken breasts, boned and skinless
2 T butter or margarine
1 package (10 ounce) frozen creamed
   spinach, thawed
1/4 cup grated parmesan cheese
1/4 cup chopped toasted pine nuts
1 T chopped fresh basil
1 clove garlic, minced
1 egg beaten with 1 T water

Preheat oven to 375°.
In medium skillet brown chicken in hot butter. Set aside.
In small bowl, combine spinach, parmesan, pine nuts,
basil, and garlic.

Roll pastry on a lightly floured board to 14 inch square.
Cut into four 7 inch squares. Spoon spinach mixture in
center of each square. Top with chicken breasts. Wrap
pastry to enclose chicken and seal. Place seam side down
on ungreased baking sheet. Brush with egg wash and
sprinkle with additional parmesan cheese.

Bake 20 minutes or until golden.

Makes 4 servings.

CHICKEN ARTICHOKE MUSHROOM SAUTÉ

4 large chicken breasts, boneless and
   skinless
flour
4 T butter
10 mushrooms, sliced
1 15 ounce can artichoke hearts, well
   drained
1/2 cup chicken stock or broth
1/4 cup white wine
juice of 1/2 lemon
salt and pepper

Dredge chicken with flour. Shake off excess. Heat butter in medium skillet. Add chicken and sauté until golden brown and cooked through. Transfer to heated platter. Add mushrooms to skillet and sauté 1 to 2 minutes. Stir in artichoke hearts, stock, wine, lemon juice, and salt and pepper to taste. Let cook until sauce is reduced slightly, stirring occasionally. Return chicken to skillet and warm through. Serve immediately.
Makes 4 servings.

PORK NORMANDY

     1 pound pork tenderloin
     2 t vegetable oil
     1 Granny Smith apple, peeled, cored
        & sliced
     12 prunes, pitted and halved
     1/2 cup Calvados or apple brandy
     1/2 cup whipping cream
     salt and pepper

Trim fat from pork and cut into 1 inch thick medallions. Pound with meat mallet or rolling pin once or twice until flattened. Heat oil in large skillet over medium-high heat. Add pork and cook until browned, 3 to 4 minutes per side. Transfer to a plate and keep warm.

To the same skillet add apple slices, prunes and 1/4 cup Calvados. Cook until apples are soft, 2 to 3 minutes. Add 1/4 cup more Calvados, 1/2 cup cream, and salt and pepper, to taste. Bring to a boil. Cook 1 minute. Return pork to pan and heat through.

Serve with couscous or rice.
Serves 4.

CHICKEN with CREAMY TARRAGON SAUCE

6 boneless, skinless half chicken
   breasts
1 carrot, sliced
1 onion, quartered
5 sprigs parsley
1 bay leaf
3 sprigs fresh thyme *or* 1/4 t dried
1 T tarragon
2 quarts chicken stock
1/2 t salt
1/4 t fresh ground pepper

Sauce
2 1/2 T butter
3 T flour
1/2 cup heavy cream
2 t tarragon

In a 4 quart Dutch oven or saucepan, combine the chicken, vegetables, herbs and stock. Bring to a boil and season with salt and pepper. Reduce heat. Cover, and simmer for about 15 minutes, or until juices run clear when pierced with a fork.

Remove the chicken pieces and strain the stock. Measure out 3 cups of the stock and set aside. Return remaining stock and chicken to Dutch oven to keep warm.

SAUCE

Place 1 cup of stock in a small saucepan. Reduce over high heat about 7 minutes, until only 2 or 3 tablespoons remain.

In another small saucepan, heat the butter. Add the flour and whisk until the mixture becomes frothy, 30 to 45 seconds. Add remaining 2 cups stock and stir with a whisk until sauce comes to a boil. Whisk for about 10 seconds. Reduce heat and simmer gently, whisking well from time to time until cosistency of heavy cream, 2 to 3 minutes.

Add the reduced stock, cream and tarragon. Bring back to a boil. Reduce the heat and simmer until sauce is consistency of heavy cream, about 10 minutes. Adjust seasoninig if necessary.

Remove chicken from poaching liquid and drain on paper towels. Place on deep serving dish and pour sauce over it.

CHICKEN POT PIE

Pastry for a two crust pie
6 boneless half-breasts of chicken
1 medium onion, diced
2 stalks celery, diced
1 egg, beaten

Sauce
1 cube butter
3 T+ flour
1 T chicken boullion
1 tsp Italian seasoning
salt and pepper to taste
1 10 ounce package frozen peas andcarrots.

Poach chicken breasts in water with onion until cooked. Remove chicken and onion from water. Reserve the liquid. Cool.
Sauté celery with a little butter in small pan. Set aside.
In a large pot, melt the cube of butter. Gradually add flour, stirring constantly, to make a roax (a thick paste). Slowly add the reserved poaching liquid, stirring constantly, until the sauce becomes the consistency of heavy cream(about 2 cups). Add salt, pepper, Italian seasoning and chicken bouillon. Mix well. Add peas and carrots, cooked celery and chicken. Pour onto prepared crust. Press along edges of pie with fork to seal. Brush with beaten egg.
Bake at 350° for about an hour or until golden brown.
When cool, cut into small chunks.
Makes 6 servings.

Note: *The pie is much easier to serve if you let it sit for about 10 minutes before cutting.*

VEGETABLES

FARMHOUSE POTATOES

1 1/2 pounds potatoes
1 cup mushrooms, sliced
1 cup Cheddar cheese, grated
1 cup whipping cream
1/4 cup butter
Salt and pepper
Parsley, chopped for garnish

Preheat oven to 400 degrees.

Peel potatoes. Cut into slices about 1/8 inch thick.
Lay potatoes on a large sheet of foil.
Cover evenly with mushrooms.
Sprinkle with cheese.
Pour on cream.
Dot with pats of butter.
Season with salt and pepper to taste.
Make a parcel of the foil. Place in a roasting pan.
Bake 1 to 1 1/2 hours until potatoes are cooked.
Serve sprinkled with parsley.
Serves 4.

GREEN BEANS with TOMATOES

4 tomatoes, peeled and chopped
2 cups green beans
3 T butter
Salt and pepper to taste
Parsley, chopped for garnish

Cook beans in boiling water.
Drain thoroughly. Turn into a serving dish. Keep warm.
Melt butter in small frying pan. Quickly sauté tomatoes.
Add salt, pepper and parsley.
Pour over beans.
Serves 4.

PEASE PUDDING

2 cups split peas
1 medium onion, finely chopped
1 t salt
2 T butter
1/2 t Worcestershire sauce
1 t pepper

Soak peas for 3 hours. Drain.
Place peas and onion in medium saucepan.
Pour over enough water just to cover.
Add 1/2 teaspoon of the salt.
Bring to a boil.
Reduce heat, cover, and simmer for 1 1/2 hours or until peas are very soft. Stir occasionally.
Drain off cooking liquid.
Purée in blender.
Return peas to pan. Cook over low heat, stirring constantly, until heated through.
Stir in butter, Worcestershire sauce, 1/2 teaspoon salt, and pepper.
Beat well to blend.
Serves 6 to 8.

BROCCOLI with SOUR CREAM

1 pound broccoli
1 T flour
1 cup sour cream,
   room temperature
2 t horseradish
1/2 t vinegar
Salt and pepper

Cook broccoli until tender. Drain thoroughly.

Mix flour and sour cream.

Put mixture into a double boiler, or into a bowl over a
pan of boiling water.

Cook until smooth, stirring constantly.

Add horseradish, vinegar, salt and pepper.

Mix well.

Pour over hot broccoli.

Serves 4.

RUMBLEDETHUMPS

2 cups cabbage, cooked
1 small onion, chopped
2 cups potatoes, cooked

Sauté onions.
Mix together cabbage, potatoes, and onion.
Fry in a little hot oil in a heavy skillet, turning to brown
on both sides.
Serves 4

May also be put into a greased casserole dish, topped
with 1 cup grated Cheddar cheese, and baked at 400
degrees until top starts to brown.

SLICED BAKED POTATOES

4 medium potatoes
1 t salt
2 to 3 T melted butter
2 to 3 T chopped fresh herbs; such as
    parsley, chives or thyme
or 2 to 3 t dried herbs of your choice
4 T grated cheddar cheese
1 1/2 parmesan cheese

Peel potatoes if skin is tough, otherwise just scrub and rinse them.

Cut potatoes into thin slices, but not all the way through.Use the handle of a spoon to prevent knife from going all the way through. Put potatoes in a baking dish. fan them slightly.

Sprinkle with salt and drizzle with butter. Sprinkle with herbs.

Bake at 425° for about 50 minutes. Remove from oven and sprinkle with cheeses. Bake for another 10 to 15 minutes until lightly browned, cheeses are melted, and potatoes are soft inside.

Makes 4 servings.

GLAZED CARROTS & PARSNIPS

1 1/2 pounds carrots and/or
    parsnips, peeled (4 cups)
2 T olive oil
1/4 cup packed brown sugar
2 T distilledwhite vinegar *or*
    balsamic vinegar *or*
    white wine vinegar
1 t cornstarch
a dash of salt

Slice carrots and/or parsnips 1/4 inch thick. Place in a medium saucepan. Add a small amount of boiling salted water. Cover and cook for 7 to 9 minutes, or until crisp-tender. Drain. Remove from pan.

In the same saucepan combine oil, brown sugar, vinegar, cornstarch, and salt. Cook until slightly thickened. Add carrots and parsnips. Cook uncovered about 2 minutes or until glazed, stirring frequently. Season to taste with pepper.
Makes 8 side dish servings.

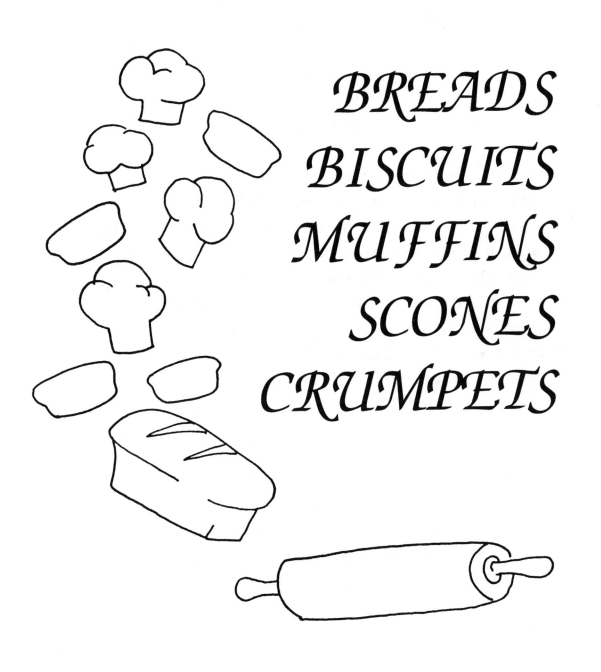

BREADS
BISCUITS
MUFFINS
SCONES
CRUMPETS

CRUMPETS

2 cups milk, scalded
1/2 cup butter
1 1/2 t salt
2 packages dry yeast
1 1/2 t sugar
3 3/4 cups flour

Combine milk, butter, and salt in a large bowl.
Stir until butter is melted. Cool to lukewarm.
Dissolve yeast in 1/4 cup warm water. Stir into milk
mixture. Stir in sugar and flour. Beat with wooden
spoon to a smooth, thick batter.
Let rise, covered, in a warm place for 1 hour, or until
doubled in bulk.
Place well-buttered crumpet rings on a well-buttered hot
griddle. A tuna can, with both top and bottom removed,
may be used if crumpet rings are not available.
Fill rings almost half full with batter. Smooth surface
with a wet spoon.
Cook over medium heat until batter has risen and
bottoms are lightly browned.
Turn crumpets and rings. Cook until browned on second
side. When serving, split in half, toast, and butter.
Makes 16 to 18 crumpets.

SCONES

6 cups flour
6 ounces raisins
3 ounces sugar
6 t baking powder
3/4 t salt
1 1/2 cubes butter or margarine,
     softened
2 cups milk

Preheat oven to 400 degrees.

Mix all ingredients together, except milk, with your hands. Add milk all at once. Mix well.
Knead mixture 8 to 10 times. Roll out on floured board to 1 1/2 inch thickness.
Cut with a biscuit cutter. Place on an ungreased cookie sheet.
Bake about 25 minutes, or until scones are lightly browned.
Serve warm with butter or clotted cream and jam.
Recipe yields about 2 dozen scones.

Scones freeze well for future use.

IRISH SODA BREAD

2 cups flour
1/2 t baking soda
2 t baking powder
1 T sugar
1/2 t salt
3 T butter or margarine, softened
1/4 cup raisins
1/4 cup currants
2 t caraway seeds
1 cup buttermilk or sour milk

Preheat oven to 350 degrees.

Sift together flour, baking soda, baking powder, sugar, and salt.
Cut in butter or margarine.
Add raisins, currants, caraway seeds, and milk. Mix thoroughly.
Turn out on a floured board. Knead 2 to 3 minutes.
Place in a greased 9 inch pie pan. Spread evenly. Cut a cross on top with a sharp, floured knife.
Bake for 30 to 45 minutes, or until golden brown.
Serve warm with butter.

DATE & WALNUT
TEA BREAD

2 cups self-rising flour
1/2 t baking powder
1 t salt
2/3 cup brown sugar
1 1/3 cups dates, pitted and chopped
1/2 cup walnuts, chopped
1 egg
5/8 cup milk

Preheat oven to 350 degrees.

Lightly grease a loaf pan.
Sift flour, baking powder, and salt into mixing bowl.
Mix in sugar, dates and walnuts.
Lightly beat egg and milk together.
Stir into flour mixture. Mix well until smooth.
Turn batter into loaf pan.
Bake for 1 to 1 1/4 hours, or until a wooden toothpick
inserted in the center comes out clean.
Cool in pan for 5 minutes. Turn onto a wire rack.
Cool before serving.

GINGERBREAD

Had I but one penny in the world, thou shouldst have it for gingerbread. **–Love's Labour's Lost**

1/2 cup butter
1/4 cup brown sugar
3 T molasses
1/2 cup maple or corn syrup
2/3 cup yogurt
2 eggs, beaten
2 cups flour
1 t allspice
3 t ginger
1/2 t baking soda

Preheat oven to 300 degrees.

Warm butter, sugar, molasses, and syrup together gently,
until butter has melted and sugar is dissolved. Cool.
Stir in yogurt and eggs.
Sift flour, allspice, ginger and baking soda into a bowl.
Add liquid mixture. Blend well.
Pour into greased and lined 7 inch square pan.
Bake for 1 1/2 hours.
When cooled, store in an airtight container.

ORANGE SCONES

3 cups flour
1/2 t baking powder
1 t baking soda
grated peel of 1/2 orange
1/4 pound butter or margarine,
      softened
3/4 cup currants or raisins
3/4 cup milk
juice of 1/2 lemon

Preheat oven to 400 degrees.
Stir together flour, sugar, baking powder, baking soda
and orange peel.
Work in butter until fine crumbs form.
Stir in raisins.
Combine milk and lemon juice. Add to mixture.
Mix until well moistened.
Scrape dough onto floured board. Knead 10 times.
Place dough into greased 9 inch pan.
Bake for approximately 40 minutes, or until lightly
browned.
Sprinkle top with sugar.
Cut into wedges.
Serve warm with butter or clotted cream.

QUEEN'S BISCUITS

1 cup flour
1 cup cheddar cheese, grated
1/2 cup butter, softened
1/2 t salt
1/2 t pepper

Preheat oven to 350 degrees.

Mix flour, salt, pepper, and cheese. Rub (mix) in butter
with hands to make a stiff paste. Chill 30 minutes.
Roll out thinly. Cut with cookie cutter. Prick with fork.
Put onto baking sheet.
Bake for 15 minutes.
Cool on a wire rack.
Store in an airtight tin.

RHUBARB MUFFINS

    2 cups rhubarb, finely chopped
    3/4 cup sugar
    1 t orange peel, grated
    2 1/2 cups flour
    1 1/2 t baking powder
    1 t baking soda
    1/2 t salt
    2 eggs, beaten
    3/4 cup buttermilk
    3 T butter or margarine, melted

Preheat oven to 375 degrees.

Combine rhubarb with 1/4 cup of sugar and orange peel.

Let stand 5 minutes.

Stir together flour, remaining 1/2 cup sugar, baking powder, baking soda, and salt.

Make a well in the center.

Combine eggs, buttermilk, and butter. Add all at once to dry ingredients, stirring just until moistened. Batter should be lumpy.

Gently fold in rhubarb mixture.

Fill greased muffin pans or paper cup liners 2/3 full.

Bake 20 to 25 minutes.

Makes 16 to 18 muffins.

HONEY MUSTARD SCONES

3 1/2 cups flour
5 t baking powder
1 t salt
3/4 cup butter or margarine,
    softened
3 eggs
1/2 cup milk
1/3 cup Dijon mustard
1/4 cup honey

Preheat oven to 425 degrees.

In large bowl, mix flour, baking powder, and salt.
With pastry blender, or hands, cut in butter or margarine
until mixture resembles coarse crumbs.
In small bowl, with wire whisk, beat 2 eggs, milk,
mustard, and honey.
Stir into flour mixture just until blended.
On lightly floured board, roll dough into 12x8 inch
rectangle.
Cut dough into eight 4x3 inch rectangles.
Cut each rectangle into 2 triangles.
Place on greased baking sheets, about 2 inches apart.
Beat remaining egg. Brush egg on scones.
Bake for about 10 minutes, or until golden brown.
Serve warm.
Makes 16 scones.

ORANGE MARMALADE BREAD

1 egg
1 cup sugar
1/3 cup butter, softened
1/3 cup milk
1/3 cup sour cream
1/3 cup orange marmalade
1 T grated lemon
    (use fruit, juice and peel)
1 1/2 cups flour
3/4 cup oatmeal
1 T baking powder
1/2 cup walnuts, chopped
1/2 cup honey

Preheat oven to 325 degrees.

Beat egg, sugar, butter, milk, sour cream, marmalade, and grated lemon together until blended.
Add flour, oatmeal, baking powder, and walnuts.
Stir until dry ingredients are just moistened.
Divide batter between four greased and lightly floured mini-loaf pans (6x3x2 inch)
Place pans on cookie sheet.
Bake for 45 to 50 minutes, or until toothpick inserted in center comes out clean.
Allow to cool for 15 minutes.
Remove from pans. Continue cooling on rack.
When cool, brush a thin layer of honey on top.
Makes 4 mini-loaves.

DATE NUT BREAD
WITH WALNUT GLAZE

2 eggs
3/4 cup orange juice
6 T butter, melted
3/4 cup sugar
1 t vanilla
1 3/4 cups flour
2 t baking powder
1/2 t baking soda
1 cup dates, pitted and chopped
1 cup walnuts, chopped

Preheat oven to 350 degrees.

Beat together eggs, orange juice, butter, sugar, and vanilla
until blended.
Add remaining ingredients.
Mix until dry ingredients are just moistened.
Scrape batter into greased and lightly floured 8x4 inch
loaf pan.
Place pan on cookie sheet. Bake for about 50 minutes, or
until toothpick inserted in center comes out clean.
Allow to cool in pan for 15 minutes. Continue to cool on
rack. When cool, drizzle with walnut glaze.

Walnut Glaze

1 T cream
2 T walnuts, finely chopped
1/2 cup powdered sugar, sifted

Stir together all ingredients until blended.

Makes 1 loaf.

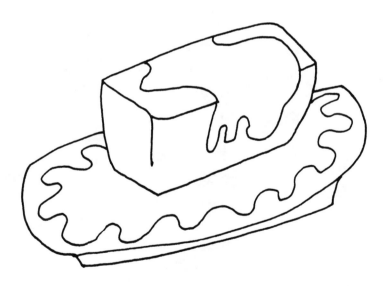

The English Rose

WHOLE WHEAT SCONES
with DATES

1 cup flour
1 cup wheat flour
2 T sugar
1/4 t salt
2 t baking powder
1/2 t baking soda

1/2 cup cold butter, cut into 8 pieces

1/2 cup buttermilk
1 egg

1 cup chopped dates

Heat oven to 425°.
In large bowl of electric mixer, stir together first 6 ingredients until well blended. Beat in the butter, until mixture resembles coarse meal. Stir together buttermilk and egg, and add to dry ingredients. On low speed, beat until well blended.Stir in the dates.

Spread batter evenly in a greased 10-inch spring form pan and bake for about 15 minutes, or until top is golden brown. Allow to cool slightly, and cut into wedges to serve.Good with clotted cream!
Makes 8 wedges.

SAVORY ONION AND CHEESE BREAD

Delicious served warm with soup or salad.

3 cups flour
4 t baking powder
3 T Parmesan cheese, grated
2 T sugar
1 t Italian herb seasoning
2 T dried onion flakes
Pinch of salt
3/4 cup milk
1 cup sour cream
1/2 cup butter, melted
1/2 cup Swiss cheese, grated

Preheat oven to 350 degrees.

Beat together all ingredients until blended. Do not over-
beat.
Spread batter evnly into oiled 9 x 13 pan.
Brush top with a little oil.
Sprinkle with additional Parmesan cheese.
Bake about 40 to 45 minutes, or until top is golden brown.
Cut into squares to serve.
Serves 8.

DESSERTS

SHORTBREAD

4 cups flour
9 ounces sugar
1 pound plus 2 ounces butter,
    softened
1/2 t salt

Preheat oven to 350 degress.

Mix together all ingredients in a large bowl.
Pat mixture firmly into a 13 x 9 pan.
Bake for about 40 minutes, or until shortbread starts to
brown around edges.
While still in pan, immediately cut into pieces about 2
inches by 1 inch.
Leave in pan until completely cooled.
Store in an air tight tin.
Makes about 24 pieces.

Shortbread freezes very well.

WALNUT SHORTBREAD

1 cup flour
1 cube butter, cut into 8 pieces
1/2 cup sugar
1 cup walnuts, shelled

Preheat oven to 350 degrees.

Put flour, butter, and sugar in a food processor. Pulse just
to mix.
Add nuts and pulse until coarsely chopped, then until
medium to coarse. The mixture should be consistency of
a coarse meal, but butter should still be visible.
Pat mixture firmly into springform pan.
Bake for 25 to 30 minutes, or until golden brown.
Remove and immediately release and remove side of pan.
Cut shortbread into 16 wedges.
Leave on bottom of pan until cold, or it will fall apart.

CHOCOLATE TOFFEE BARS

3/4 cup butter or margarine,
   softened
1/2 cup sugar
1 1/2 cups flour

Topping:
1/2 cup butter or margarine
1/4 cup sugar
2 T light corn syrup
2/3 cup sweetened condensed milk
4 ounces semi sweet chocolate
1 T shortening

Preheat oven to 325 degrees.

Lightly grease an 8 or 9 inch square baking pan.
In a medium bowl, beat butter or margarine and sugar 5
to 8 minutes, or until light and fluffy.
Stir in flour to make a smooth dough.
Knead dough in bowl 8 to 10 strokes.
Pat out dough evenly in bottom of greased pan. Prick
dough with a fork.
Bake in preheated oven 35 to 40 minutes or until golden.
Cool in pan on a wire rack.

Topping

In a medium saucepan over low heat, combine butter or margarine, sugar, corn syrup and condensed milk.
Cook, stirring constantly, until mixture comes to a boil.
Boil 5 to 7 minutes, or until mixture is toffee-colored and thickened. Stir occasionally. Cool slightly.
Spread over cooled shortbread in pan.
Let stand until cool.
In a small heavy saucepan, over very low heat, melt chocolate and shortening.
Cook, stirring until smooth. Cool slightly.

Spread chocolate over cooled toffee.
Let stand until chocolate is set.
Cut into bars. Remove from pan.
Makes 20 bars.

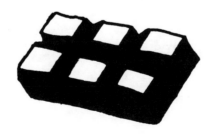

FLAPJACKS
Delicious and moist oatmeal squares

6 T butter, softened
2 T brown sugar
1/8 t salt
1/4 t ground ginger
3 T corn syrup
1 T honey
1 1/2 cups rolled oats

Preheat oven to 375 degrees.

Grease 8 inch square pan.
Cream butter and sugar together with wooden spoon.
Add salt, ginger, syrup, and honey.
Beat until smooth and creamy.
Stir in oats.
Press mixture into pan, smoothing it down with the back of knife.
Bake for 25 minutes, or until lightly browned and firm to the touch.
Cut into squares.
Let cool before serving.
Makes 9 flapjacks.

BERNIE'S FRUITCAKE

1 pound walnuts, chopped
1/2 pound Brazil nuts or pecans,
   chopped
3/4 pound moist dates, chopped
1 cup candied maraschino cherries
3/4 cup sugar
3/4 cup flour
1 t salt
1 t baking powder
3 eggs, beaten
1 t vanilla

Preheat oven to 325 degress.

Grease and line a 3x4x8 inch loaf pan with waxed paper.

Mix all ingredients except eggs and vanilla in large bowl
until well coated.
Add eggs and vanilla. Mix well.
Bake for one hour and 35 minutes.
Cover with foil for the last 45 minutes to avoid crusting.
Makes one loaf.

MAIDS of HONOR BARS

        1 1/2 cups flour
        1/4 cup sugar
        3/4 cup butter, softened
        1/2 cup almonds, finely chopped
        1 egg, beaten
        3/4 cup apricot jam, sieved

Preheat oven to 350 degrees.

In a large bowl, beat together flour, sugar, and butter
until mixture resembles coarse meal.
Beat in almonds.
Add egg. Beat until a dough forms. Do not overbeat.
Pat mixture on bottom and 1/2 inch up sides of greased
9x13 inch baking pan.
Bake 20 minutes, or until top is very lightly browned.
Spread apricot jam evenly over top.

Almond filling

        1 package (7 ounces) almond paste
        1/2 cup sugar
        1 T flour
        2 eggs
        2 T cream
        1 t almond extract

Beat together all ingredients until blended.

Spread mixture evenly over almond cookie crust.

Bake at 350 degrees for about 25 minutes, or until topping is set and browned.

Allow to cool in pan. When cool, cut into 1 1/2 inch squares.

Sprinkle with powdered sugar.

Makes 4 dozen bars.

ICED ORANGE SQUARES

3/4 cup butter or margarine,
  softened
1 1/4 cups sugar
3 eggs
2 1/2 cups flour
1 1/2 t baking soda
1 1/4 cups orange juice
1 T orange peel, grated

Icing:
1 1/4 cups powdered sugar, sifted
3 T orange juice

Preheat oven to 350 degrees.

Grease and flour a 13 x 9 baking pan.

In large bowl, beat butter or margarine, sugar, eggs, flour, baking soda, orange juice, and orange peel with electric mixer at low speed 1 minute, or until blended.
Increase speed to high. Beat 3 minutes, scraping down sides of bowl occasionally.
Pour batter into prepared pan. Smooth top.
Bake 45 to 50 minutes, or until wooden toothpick inserted in center comes out clean.
Cool in pan on wire rack for 15 minutes.

Icing

In a small bowl, beat powdered sugar and orange juice
until smooth.
Spoon icing over top of warm cake in pan.
Cool iced cake completely in pan on wire rack.

Cut into squares. Remove from pan.
Makes 18 to 24 squares.

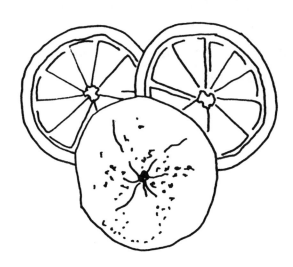

LEMON SLICES

2 cups flour
1/2 cup powdered sugar
1 cup butter, softened

Topping
4 eggs
2 cups sugar
1 t baking powder
Juice of 4 lemons
Grated peel of two lemons
Dash of salt

Preheat oven 350 degrees.

Sift flour and powdered sugar into a bowl.
Blend in softened butter.
Pat mixture into 13x9 pan.
Bake for 20 minutes.

Topping:

Beat eggs.
Add remaining ingredients.
Mix well.

Pour topping mixture over baked shortbread.
Bake for 25 to 30 minutes, or until the edges begin to brown.
Cool in the pan on a wire rack.
Cut into pieces. Sprinkle with powdered sugar.
Makes 8 large bars.

These freeze very well.

HONEY BAKED APPLES

4 cooking apples
1/3 cup lemon juice
1/2 cup honey
1 t cinnamon or 4 whole cloves
2 T butter

Preheat oven to 350 degrees.

Wipe apples. Core.
Arrange close together in a greased shallow oven proof dish.
Mix honey and lemon juice.
Pour over apples.
Sprinkle with cinnamon, or add cloves.
Dot with butter.
Bake at 350 degrees for 25 minutes.
Serve hot with cream.
Serves 4.

BAKED PEARS in WHITE WINE

6 T orange marmalade

6 T macaroons, coarsely crushed

6 large ripe pears, peeled,
   halved and cored

1 cup sweet white wine

3 T butter or margarine

Preheat oven to 350 degrees.

Grease shallow oven proof dish large enough to hold
pears in a single layer.
In a small bowl, blend marmalade and macaroons.
Place pear halves in greased dish, cut side up.
Fill pears with marmalade mixture.
Pour wine over pears.
Dot pears with butter.
Bake for 20 to 30 minutes, or until tender when tested
with wooden toothpick. Serve warm or at room
temperature.
Serves 6.

STRAWBERRIES IN BUTTERSCOTCH SAUCE

1 1/2 pounds fresh strawberries,
washed and hulled

Sauce
1 cup light brown sugar, packed
1 cup corn syrup
1/2 cup whipping cream
3 or 4 drops of vanilla

Place strawberries in individual serving dishes.

Sauce
Combine brown sugar and corn syrup in medium
saucepan.
Stir over low heat until sugar dissolves.
Cook for 5 minutes.
Remove from heat.
Stir in cream and vanilla.
Beat about 2 minutes, or until sauce is smooth.
Top strawberries with warm sauce.
Serves 4.

Variation
Make sauce ahead. Refrigerate. Do not reheat.
Serve chilled.

TIPSY BANANAS

1 banana
1 T fresh orange juice
1 T sherry
Brown sugar
Whipped cream

Slice banana lengthwise.
Put cut side up in an oven proof dish.
Pour orange juice and sherry over halves.
Sprinkle with brown sugar.
Put under broiler until banana has softened and sugar is bubbling.
Serve with cream if desired.
Serves 1.

DAPHNE'S RUM CAKE

1 cup nuts, chopped
1 package yellow cake mix
1 package vanilla
   instant pudding mix
4 eggs
1/2 cup water
1/2 cup rum
1/2 cup oil

Glaze
1/4 cup butter
1/4 cup water
1 cup sugar
1/2 cup rum

Preheat oven to 325 degrees.

Grease and flour a bundt pan or angel food pan.
Sprinkle nuts in bottom of pan.
Mix remaining ingredients well. Pour into pan over nuts.
Bake for one hour.
Cool. Invert onto serving plate.

Glaze

Melt butter.
Stir in water and sugar.
Boil for 5 minutes, stirring constantly.
Remove from heat.
Stir in rum.

Drizzle glaze evenly over top and sides.

PECAN SLICES

1 package yellow cake mix
1/2 cup butter or margarine,
    softened
2 eggs
1 14 ounce can condensed milk
1 t vanilla
1 cup pecans, chopped
1/2 cup butterscotch morsels or
    Heath Bar Bits

Preheat oven to 350 degrees.

In a bowl combine cake mix, butter, and 1 egg.
Mix at low speed until crumbly.
Press into 13x9 pan.
In a small bowl, beat condensed milk, one egg, and
vanilla until blended.
Stir in pecans and butterscotch morsels.
Pour over cake mixture.
Bake at 350 degrees for 25 to 30 minutes.
Cool before cutting into squares.
Makes 8 large slices.

CHOCOLATE CAKE

1 package Supermoist Devil's
  Food cake mix
1 cup mayonnaise
3 eggs
1 cup water

Frosting
3 ounces cream cheese, softened
1 cube butter, softened
6 t cocoa powder
2 cups powdered sugar, sifted
1 cup raspberry jam (optional)

Preheat oven to 350 degrees.

Prepare cake according to package directions, substituting above ingredients.

Pour mixture into 3 cake pans, or two pans if you prefer.

Bake for approximately 25 minutes, or until cake springs back to the touch.

Let cool before frosting.

Frosting
Mix cream cheese and butter with cocoa.
Add powdered sugar slowly until frosting is a smooth consistency.
Raspberry jam may be spread between each layer when frosting.

APPLE CRACKLE CAKE

2 cups flour

2 t baking powder

Pinch of salt

1 t cinnamon

1/2 t nutmeg

1/2 cup butter or margarine,
   softened

1/2 cup sugar

1/2 pound green cooking apples,
   finely sliced

2 eggs

1/2 cup milk

Topping

3 T sugar

1   butter or margarine

Preheat oven to 375 degrees.

Sift flour with baking powder.

Add salt, cinnamon, and nutmeg.

Rub (mix) butter or margarine in with hands.

Stir in sugar and apples.

Mix to a thick batter with eggs and milk.

Stir until smooth.

Turn into well greased 8 inch round cake pan.

Cover top with sugar and small pieces of butter or margarine.

Bake at 375 degrees for 45 minutes. Lower heat to 325 degrees. Bake an additional 30 minutes. Serve warm with cream or ice cream.

TREACLE TART

The Queen of Hearts,
She made some tarts,
All on a summer's days.
—Nursery Rhyme

1 8 inch tart shell, baked and
   cooled
Grated rind of small lemon
2 t lemon juice
3/4 cup golden syrup or
     light corn syrup
3/4 cup fresh white bread crumbs
     or crushed cornflakes

Preheat oven to 375 degrees.

Place tart shell on baking sheet.
Put lemon rind in top of double boiler.
Add lemon juice and syrup.
Mix together thoroughly.
Heat until syrup is softened.
Stir in bread crumbs or corn flakes.
Spoon mixture into pastry shell.
Bake 20 minutes or until golden brown.

TRIFLE

1 10 ounce container frozen
    raspberries, defrosted or fresh
    raspberries when available
2 1/2 cups milk
4 level T Bird's custard powder
4 T sugar
1 small pound cake
Slivered almonds
Cream sherry
1/2 pint whipped cream

Cover bottom of tall glass serving dish with slices of
pound cake, cut about 1/2 inch thick.
Soak with sherry.
Pour over raspberries, including juice.
Distribute evenly over cake.
Sprinkle with almonds.

To make custard, put 2 cups milk in a saucepan. Heat to
almost boiling point.
Meanwhile, mix remaining 1/2 cup milk with custard
powder and sugar.
Pour into hot milk, stirring constantly. Keep cooking for
2 to 3 minutes, until custard is thick and creamy.

Pour over cake and raspberries.
Cover with plastic wrap.
Chill about two hours, or until custard is set.
Just before serving, top with whipped cream.
Serves 4 to 6.

SHERRY SPICE CAKE with SHERRY GLAZE

1/2 cup butter, softened
1 cup brown sugar
1 egg
1/2 cup cream sherry
2 T orange juice
1 T orange peel, grated
2 cups flour
2 t baking powder
1/2 t baking soda
3/4 cup raisins
3/4 cup walnuts, chopped
3/4 cup dark currants or raisins
2 t pumpkin pie spice
1 t vanilla

Sherry glaze
1 T cream sherry
1/2 cup powdered sugar, sifted

Preheat oven 325 degrees.

Beat together first 5 ingredients until blended.
Add remaining ingredients.
Beat until blended.
Spread batter into greased 10 inch tube pan.

Bake for about 50 minutes, or until a wooden tooth pick inserted in center comes out clean.

Cool in pan.

When cool, brush top with sherry glaze.

To make sherry glaze, stir sherry and powdered sugar together until blended.

Serves 10.

BUTTERSCOTCH CUSTARD

1 cup brown sugar
6 T flour
3 cups milk
3 eggs, separated
3/4 t vanilla

Mix sugar and flour together thoroughly.
Slowly add milk, stirring until smooth.
Cook over boiling water 15 minutes.
While mixture is cooking, beat egg yolks.
Beat whites until stiff. Set aside.
Stir small amount of hot mixture into egg yolks.
Return to remaining hot mixture.
Cool two minutes longer, stirring constantly.
Remove from heat.
Gently fold mixture into egg whites.
Add vanilla.
Spoon into dessert glasses.
Refrigerate until chilled.
Serves 6.

BAKEWELL TART

1 8 inch tart shell, uncooked
2 T raspberry jam
2 eggs, separated
1 1/2 cups fresh bread crumbs
3/8 cup sugar
4 T butter, melted
2/3 cup almonds, ground
Grated rind of 1 lemon
Juice of 1 lemon
Pinch of salt

Preheat oven to 425 degrees.

Spread a layer of jam on bottom of pastry shell.
Put egg yolks in a medium bowl. Beat well.
Add bread crumbs, sugar, butter, almonds, lemon rind,
and lemon juice. Mix well.
Beat egg whites with salt until stiff.
Fold into egg yolk mixture.
Spread mixture over jam.
Bake for 30 minutes, or until filling is firm and lightly
browned.

HONEY, APPLE & ALMOND PUDDING

1 pound green cooking apples,
   peeled, cored and sliced
4 T honey
1 cup fresh bread crumbs
6 T butter or margarine
1/2 cup sugar
1/2 almonds, ground
1 egg, beaten

Preheat oven to 375 degreees.

Stew apples with honey and a little water until soft.
Stir in bread crumbs.
Turn mixture into buttered oven proof dish.
Melt butter over low heat.
Mix with sugar, almonds, and egg.
Spread over apple mixture.
Bake at 375 degrees for 45 minutes.
Serve with whipped cream.
Serves 4.

QUICK CHOCOLATE MOUSSE

6 ounces semi sweet chocolate
   chips
5 T boiling water
4 eggs, separated
2 T Grand Marnier or sherry
Dash of cream of tartar
Grated peel of 1 orange

Chop chocolate chips in blender on high for 6 seconds.
Add boiling water. Blend for 10 seconds.
Add egg yolks and liqueur.
Blend about 3 seconds until smooth.
Beat egg whites with cream of tartar in medium bowl
until stiff, but not dry.
Gently fold into chocolate mixture, along with orange
peel.
Divide among dessert dishes. Cover with plastic wrap.
Refrigerate at least one hour.
Serves 6.

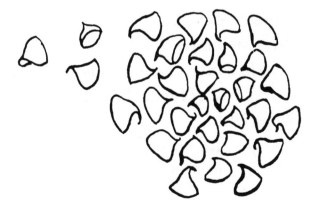

BREAD & APPLE PUDDING

8 slices white bread, 1/4 inch thick
3 T butter
1 1/2 pounds green cooking apples
6 T brown sugar
1 t cinnamon
3 eggs
1 1/4 cups milk
Extra brown sugar for topping

Preheat oven to 350 degrees.

Cut crusts off bread.
Using 2 tablespoons of the butter, spread each slice on one side only.
Cut each slice into 4 squares.
Peel, core and slice apples.
Put half the apples into lightly buttered oven proof casserole dish.
Mix sugar and cinnamon. Sprinkle 1/3 over apples.
Cover with half the bread and another 1/3 of sugar and cinnamon mixture.
Add remaining apples.
Sprinkle with remaining sugar and cinnamon.
Overlap rest of bread, butter side up, in a circle around edge of dish.
Beat eggs and milk together. Pour over top.
Sprinkle with brown sugar.

Cover. Bake at 350 degrees for 30 minutes.
Melt remaining tablespoon of butter. Brush over apple in center.
Bake uncovered for an additional 30 minutes until bread is golden brown.
Serves 6.

PECAN PIE

1 10 inch pie shell, uncooked
1 cup white corn syrup
1 cup dark brown sugar
1/3 cup butter, melted
2 1/2 cups pecans, shelled
3 eggs, beaten
Dash of vanilla
Pinch of salt

Preheat oven to 350 degrees.

Mix all ingrerdients well.
Pour into pie shell.
Bake at 350 degrees for 45 to 50 minutes, or until crust is browned.
Cool before serving.
Serves 6.

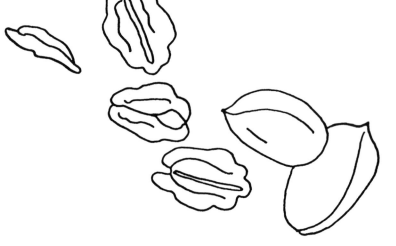

LEMON POSSET

2 2/3 cups whipping cream
Juice of 2 lemons
Grated rind of 2 lemons
2/3 cup dry white wine
Sugar to taste
3 eggs, whites only

Add lemon rind to whipping cream. Whip until stiff.
Stir in lemon juice and wine.
Add sugar to taste.
Whip egg whites until they form peaks.
Fold into whipped cream mixture.
Serve in individual glasses or glass serving dish.
Serves 4.

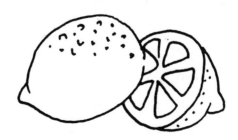

LEMON POUND CAKE

1 cup butter or margarine, softened
1 1/2 cups sugar
6 eggs
Juice of 2 lemons
Grated peel of 2 lemons
1 1/2 cups flour
1 T baking powder
1 t salt
3/4 cup milk
Powdered sugar

Preheat oven to 350 degrees.
Grease and flour 12 cup bundt pan.

In a large bowl, beat butter or margarine and sugar 5 to 8
minutes, or until light and fluffy.
Beat in eggs, one at a time, beating well after each
addition.
Beat in lemon peel and juice until blended.
Sift flour, baking powder, and salt into medium bowl.
Add flour mixture to sugar mixture alternately with milk.
Beat until blended.
Pour batter into pan. Smooth top.
Bake in oven 55 to 60 minutes, or until a wooden
toothpick inserted in center comes out clean.
Cool in pan on wire rack for 10 minutes.

Remove from pan.
Cool on wire rack.
Place on serving plate.
Sift powdered sugar over top before serving.
Serves 12 to 18.

NORFOLK SYLLABUB

1/2 cup white wine
1 T sherry
3 T brandy
1 lemon
1/4 cup sugar
1 1/4 cups whipping cream

Put wine, sherry, and brandy into small bowl.
Peel lemon very thinly and squeeze out juice.
Put peel and juice into wine mixture.
Leave overnight.
Remove peel.
Stir in sugar until it dissolves.
Add cream.
Whip until mixture forms soft peaks.
Put into dessert glasses.
Serves 4.

GOOSEBERRY FOOL

2 cups canned sweetened
  gooseberries, drained
1/2 cup sugar
3/4 cup whipping cream
1 egg white

In blender process gooseberries until puréed.
Press purée through sieve to remove seeds.
Stir in 6 tablespoons sugar.
Refrigerate until chilled.
In a medium bowl, whip cream until stiff peaks form.
In a small bowl, beat egg white until stiff peaks form.
Gradually beat in remaining sugar. Beat until stiff.
Fold beaten egg white mixture into whipped cream.
Fold gooseberry purée into cream mixture.
If desired, spoon a few gooseberries into glasses before
adding fool.
Spoon into 4 wine or sherbert glasses.
Refrigerate until chilled.
Serves 4.

STEAMED FUDGE PUDDING

1　6 ounce package semi sweet
　　chocolate pieces
4　eggs, slightly beaten
2　cups milk
1/2　cup brown sugar, packed
3/4　t cinnamon
1/4　t salt
4　cups dry bread cubes
1/2　cup nuts, chopped
　　Whipped cream (optional)

Preheat oven to 350 degrees.

Melt chocolate pieces.
In a large mixing bowl, combine eggs, milk, brown sugar,
cinnamon, salt, and melted chocolate.
Stir in bread cubes and nuts.
Turn mixture into ungreased 10x6x2 inch baking dish.
Place baking dish into a 13x9x2 inch baking pan.
Set on oven rack.
Pour boiling water into large pan to a depth of 1 inch. Be
careful not to spill any water into chocolate mixture.
Bake, uncovered, for 60 to 65 minutes, or until a knife
inserted near the center of pudding comes out clean.
Cut into squares.
Serve pudding warm. If desired, top with whipped cream.
Serves 8.

ENGLISH ROSE BLACKBERRY & APPLE CRUMBLE

8 large green cooking apples
1 pound fresh or frozen
   blackberries
4 T brown sugar
2 t cinnamon

Topping
2 cups flour
1 cup sugar
1 cup butter or margarine, softened

Preheat oven to 350 degrees.

Peel and slice apples. Put in 15x9x3 baking pan.
Cover with blackberries.
Sprinkle with brown sugar and cinnamon.
Mix together ingredients for topping. Spread evenly over fruit in pan.
Bake for approximately 45 minutes , or until
golden brown.
Serves 8.

STICKY TOFFEE PUDDING

This rich, creamy dessert is featured at Sheila's Cottage in Ambleside, England. We appreciate being able to share it with you.

1 cup plus 1 T flour
1 t baking powder
3/4 cup dates, pitted and finely
    chopped
7 T unsalted butter
3/4 cup sugar
1 egg, lightly beaten
1 t baking soda
1 t vanilla
1 1/4 cups boiling water
5 T brown sugar, packed
2 T heavy cream
Whipped cream

Preheat oven to 350 degrees.
Butter an 8x6 inch baking dish. Make certain dish is broiler proof.

Sift flour and baking powder into bowl. Set aside.
Toss dates with 1 tablespoon flour in small bowl.
Beat 4 tablespoons butter and the sugar in large bowl until mixture is light and fluffy.
Beat in egg, along with a little of flour mixture. Beat for 1 minute.

Beat in remaining flour mixture.

Add dates, baking soda, and vanilla to boiling water, stirring to combine.

Add to batter. Beat until well blended.

Pour batter into baking dish.

Bake until set and well browned on top, 30 to 40 minutes.

Remove from oven. Place on wire rack.

Heat broiler.

Heat remaining butter, brown sugar, and heavy cream in small saucepan over medium heat to simmering. Simmer about 3 minutes, or until thickened. Remove from heat.

Pour topping over hot pudding.

Place pudding in broiler, about 4 inches from source of heat.

Broil about 1 minute, or until topping is bubbling.

Serve hot or warm, accompanied by whipped cream.

Serves 6 to 8.

PETTICOAT TAILS

The English modified the French name of *petits gateaux taillés* for these cookies to Petticoat Tails.

Preheat oven to 350 degrees.

> 1 cup butter
> 3/4 cup sugar
> 1 egg, well beaten
> 1 T cream
> 4 cups flour
> 1/4 t salt

Cream butter and sugar thoroughly.
Add egg, cream, flour and salt.
Knead until smooth on floured board.
Roll out into large round.
Cut out small round from center.
Divide remaining portion into eight pieces.
Pinch edges. Mark all over with fork.
Place on greased baking sheet.
Bake for 15 minutes.

CARROT & PECAN TORTE
with ORANGE SYRUP

4 eggs
1 cup sugar
2 cups pecans
2 medium carrots, cut into 1-inch pieces
peel of 1 orange(just the orange zest,
not the white pith)

1 cup flour
1 t baking powder
2 t cinnamon

Orange Syrup
3 T orange juice
1/2 cup sifted powdered sugar

Preheat oven to 350°.

Put first 5 ingredients in bowl of food processor, and blend until finely chopped(not pureed) or, chop all by hand until finely chopped, and mix together. Add remaining ingredients and mix until blended.

Spread batter into a greased 10-inch spring form pan and bake for about 30 minutes, or until toothpick inserted in center comes out clean. Spoon orange syrup over the hot torte.

Allow to cool in pan and cut into wedges.

Makes 10 servings.

APPLE CAKE
with
ORANGE & NUTS

1 orange, peeled & cut into small
  pieces
2 cups nuts (walnuts or pecans)
2 large apples (peeled, cored &
  chopped into small pieces)

4 eggs
2 cups sugar
4 t vanilla
1 1/3 cups flour
4 t baking powder

Creamy Raisin Glaze
2 T cream
2 cups powdered sugar
4 T finely chopped raisins
1 t vanilla

Combine all the ingredients in a large bowl. Blend well.
Pour into a buttered 9 x13 inch pan. Bake at 350° for 30 to
45 minutes, or until browned and a knife, inserted in
center, comes out clean. Allow to cool in pan.

When cool, top with creamy raisin glaze. Cut in squares
to serve.

Creamy Raisin Glaze

Stir together all ingredients until blended. Add a little more cream if necessary to make glaze a drizzling consisitency.

Store in refrigerator. Good served with whipped cream too!

STRAWBERRY JAM &
ALMOND CAKE
with
STRAWBERRY GLAZE

1/2 cup of butter
3/4 cup sugar
2 eggs

1/2 cup strawberry jam
1/4 cup sour cream
1 t almond extract

1 1/2 cups flour
1 t baking powder
1/2 t baking soda
1/2 cup chopped toasted almonds

Strawberry Glaze
2 T strawberry jam
1 T cream
2/3 cup sifted powdered sugar

Preheat oven to 360 degrees.

Cream butter with sugar, until mixture is light. Beat in eggs until thoroughly blended. Beat in jam, sour cream and almond extract until blended. Combine and add the remaining ingredients and beat until mixture is blended.

Spread batter in a greased 10-inch tube pan and bake for 35 to 40 minutes, or until toothpick, inserted in center, comes out clean. Allow to cool in pan. When cool, remove from pan. Brush top with strawberry glaze and allow a little to drip down sides.

Strawberry Glaze

Stir together all ingredients until blended.
Serves 8 to 10.

CARAMEL PEAR UPSIDE-DOWN CAKE

1 29 ounce can pear halves

1 12 ounce jar caramel topping
1 package pudding-included yellow
   cake mix
1 cup water
1/3 cup oil
3 eggs
1/4 cup chopped nuts
whipped cream, if desired

Heat oven to 350°.
Generously grease 13x9 inch pan. Slice pear halves.
Arrange over bottom of pan. Pour caramel topping over
all.(Heat topping in microwave to soften, if necessary).

In large bowl, combine cake mix, water, oil and eggs at
low speed until moistened. Beat 2 minutes at high speed.
Spoon batter evenly over pear mixture.

Bake for 35 to 55 minutes, or until toothpick inserted in
center comes out clean. Cool 5 minutes. Turn onto serving
platter. Sprinkle with nuts. Serve warm with whipped
cream, if desired.
Makes 12 servings.

OATMEAL CARMELITAS

Crust
2 cups all-purpose flour
2 cups quick cooking oats
1 1/2 cups firmly packed brown
  sugar
1 t baking soda
1/2 t salt
1 1/4 cups margarine or butter,
  softened

Filling
1 cup caramel topping
3 T flour
1 cup semi-sweet chocolate chips
1/2 cup chopped nuts

Heat oven to 350°. Grease 13x9 inch pan. In a large bowl, blend all crust ingredients at low speed until crumbly. Press half of mixture, about 3 cups, in bottom of pan. Bake for 10 minutes. Meanwhile, in small bowl, combine caramel topping aand 3 tablespoons flour. Sprinkle cooked crust with chocolate and nuts. Drizzle evenly with caramel mixture. Sprinkle with reserved crumb mixture. Bake for an additional 18 to 22 minutes or until golden brown. Cool completely. Refrigerate 1 to 2 hours until filling is set. Cut into bars.
Makes 12 bars.

SOUR CREAM LEMON PIE

9 inch pie crust shell

Filling
1 cup sugar
3 T cornstarch
1 cup milk
1/4 cup lemon juice
3 egg yolks, slightly beaten
1/4 cup butter or margarine,
   softened
1 T grated lemon peel
1 cup sour cream

Heat oven to 450°. Bake crust for 9 to 11 minutes, or until golden brown. Cool.

In medium saucepan, combine sugar and cornstarch. Blend well. Stir in milk, lemon juice and egg yolks. Cook over medium heat, stirring constantlyuntil thick. Remove from heat. Stir in margarine and lemon peel. Cool slightly. Fold in sour cream. Spoon into cooked baked shell. Refrigerate at least two hours or until set.
Makes 8 servings.

BANANA TIRAMISU

1 1/2 cups milk

2 T instant coffee

18 ounce package cream cheese, softened

1/4 cup sugar

1 package vanilla instant pudding & pie filling

2 cups nondairy whipped topping, thawed

3 medium, ripe bananas, sliced

6 ounces lady fingers, split and cut in half *or* 1 10 ounce prepared sponge cake

1 1/2 ouces semisweet chocolate, grated

Stir together milk and coffee until coffee is almost dissolved. Beat together cream cheese and sugar in large bowl until smooth and blended. Add pudding mix. Gradually beat in coffee mixture until smooth and blended. Gently stir in whipped topping and sliced bananas until just blended.

Layer one-third of lady fingers (or sponge cake) on bottom of 9x13 dish. Evenly spoon one-third of the cream mixture and sprinkle with half the grated chocolate. Repeat layers, ending with cream mixture. Chill at least one hour before serving. Garnish with additional sliced bananas and chocolate if desired. Serves 12.

RASPBERRY TOPPED LEMON PIE

3 egg yolks
1 14 ounce can sweetened condensed
  milk
1/2 cup lemon juice
1 6 ounce graham cracker
  crust
1 10 ounce package frozen
  raspberries in syrup, thawed
1 T cornstarch

Preheat oven to 375°. Brush bottom and sides of crust with beaten egg white. Bake about 5 minutes, or until lightly browned.

Lower oven to 325°. With mixer, beat egg yolks and condensed milk until well blended. Stir in lemon juice. Pour into crust. Bake 30 minutes.

Meanwhile, in saucepan, combine raspberries ands cornstarch. Cook and stir until mixture thickens and is clear. Spoon on top of pie.

Chill at least 4 hours. Top with whipped cream if desired. Refrigerate leftovers.

CARAMEL APPLE PIE

1 12 ounce package escalloped
   apples, defrosted
6 ounce cream cheese, softened
1 egg
1 1/2 t vanilla
3 T sugar
1 T flour
1 6 ounce graham cracker crust
1/3 cup caramel topping
1/2 t cinnamon

Preheat oven to 375°. In a mixing bowl combine softened cream cheese, egg, vanilla, sugar and flour. Beat until smooth. Spread mixture over pie crust. Combine apples, caramel topping and cinnamon. Gently spoon over cream cheese mixture to keep two distinct layers.
Bake for 40-45 minutes or until apples bubble up around edge of pie.
Serve at room temperature.
Store leftover pie in fridge.

LIME CREAM TORTE

Cake

1 package pudding-included butter
    flavor cake mix
2 T lime juice plus water to equal
    1 cup
1/2 cup butter, softened
3 eggs

Filling

1 (14 ounce) can sweetened
    condensed milk
1/2 cup lime juice
2 cups whipping cream

Heat oven to 350°. Grease and flour two 8 or 9-inch round
cake pans. In large bowl, combine all cake ingredients at
low speed until moistened. Beat 2 minutes at high speed.
Pour batter into pans. Bake 9-inch pans 20 to 30 minutes;
8-inch pans 30 to 40 minutes, or until toothpick inserted
in center comes out clean. Cool 15 minutes. Remove from
pans. Cool completely.

In a small bowl, combine condensed milk and lime juice.
Mix well. In a large bowl, beat whipping cream until stiff
peaks form. Reserve 1 cup of whipped cream. Fold

condensed milk mixture into remaining whipped cream just until blended.

Slice each cake layer in half to make 4 layers. Place a layer cut side up on plate. Spread with 1/3 of whipped cream filling. Repeat with second and third layers. Top with remaining cake layer. Spread reserved whipped cream over top of torte. Refrigerate 2 to 3 hours before serving. Garnish with lime slices.

Makes 12 servings.

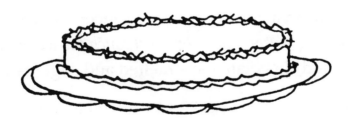

JACKIE'S BREAD PUDDING

9 slices white bread
5 ounces dark chocolate
15 fluid ounces whipping cream
4 T dark rum
4 ounces sugar
3 ounces butter
good pinch of cinnamon
3 large eggs
thick pouring cream, well chilled, to
pour over pudding

Remove crusts from bread. Cut all slices into 4 triangles. Place chocolate, whipping cream, rum, sugar, butter, and cinnamon in a bowl. Set over a saucepan over barely simmering water. *Don't let bowl touch the water.* Wait until butter and chocolate have melted and sugar is dissolved.

Remove bowl from heat and stir well to amalgamate all ingredients.

Whisk eggs in a separate bowl. Pour the chocolate mixture over them and whisk again, very well, to blend together.

Spoon about 1/2 inch layer of chocolate mixture into base of a lightly buttered, 7x9x2 ovenproof dish. Arrange half of bread triangle over the chocolate in overlapping rows. Now pour 1/2 of remaining chocolate mixture all over the bread, as evenly as possible. Arrange the rest of the triangles over that. Finish off with a layer of chocolate. Use a fork to press the bread gently down so that it gets covered very evenly with liquid as it cools. Cover the dish with plastic wrap and allow to stand at room temperature for two hours. Then transfer to refrigerator for 48 hours.

Before cooking, heat oven to 350°. Remove plastic wrap. Put pudding in oven for 30-35 minutes or until top is crunchy and inside is soft and springy.

Leave to stand 10 minutes before serving.

Serve with well chilled heavy cream.

Serves 8.

A POT OF TEA

Heat teapot by filling with hot water.
Let stand for a few minutes.
Bring freshly drawn cold water to a rolling boil.
Do not overboil because   that expels oxygen from the water.
Empty hot water from teapot.
Put in one teaspoon loose tea in a tea caddy, or one teabag, for each two cup serving.
Pour on freshly boiled water. Allow to brew for 3 to 5 minutes. Use a tea strainer if using loose tea.
Keep tea in teapot warm under a tea cosy.
Serve with milk or lemon.

The English Rose

Marilyn Sheppard

Marilyn Haslett Sheppard was born in Enfield, Middlesex — just north of London. She left England with her parents and brother when she was five years old. They settled in the Bay Area, where she has lived ever since. Marilyn has always retained her ties with England, returning there many times to visit relatives, explore the countryside, and savor the food.

Her ongoing interest in cooking led to her first experience with restaurant life. She and her aunt, Joyce Thomas, opened an English Tea Shop. Encouraged by its great success they decided to open another in San Carlos, California.

In its 16 years of existence, **The English Rose Restaurant** has become very well known on the San Francisco Peninsula for its delicious food, friendly atmosphere, and English decor.

Marilyn resides in Belmont with her husband Steve, and two children.